Emoji Coloring Book For Girls (and unicorns)

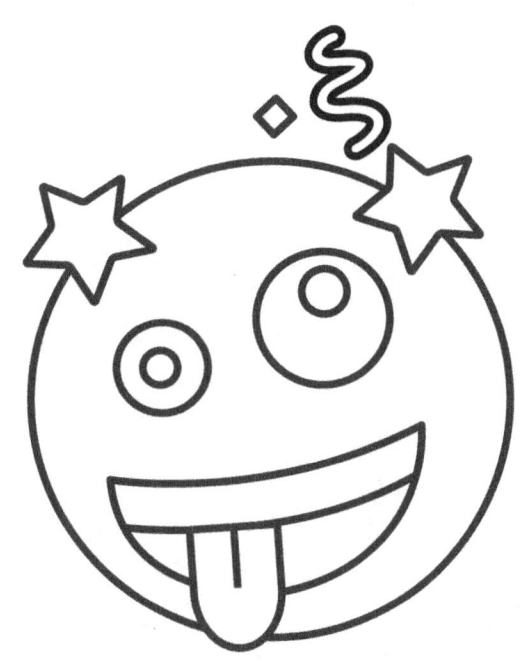

By

Dani Kates

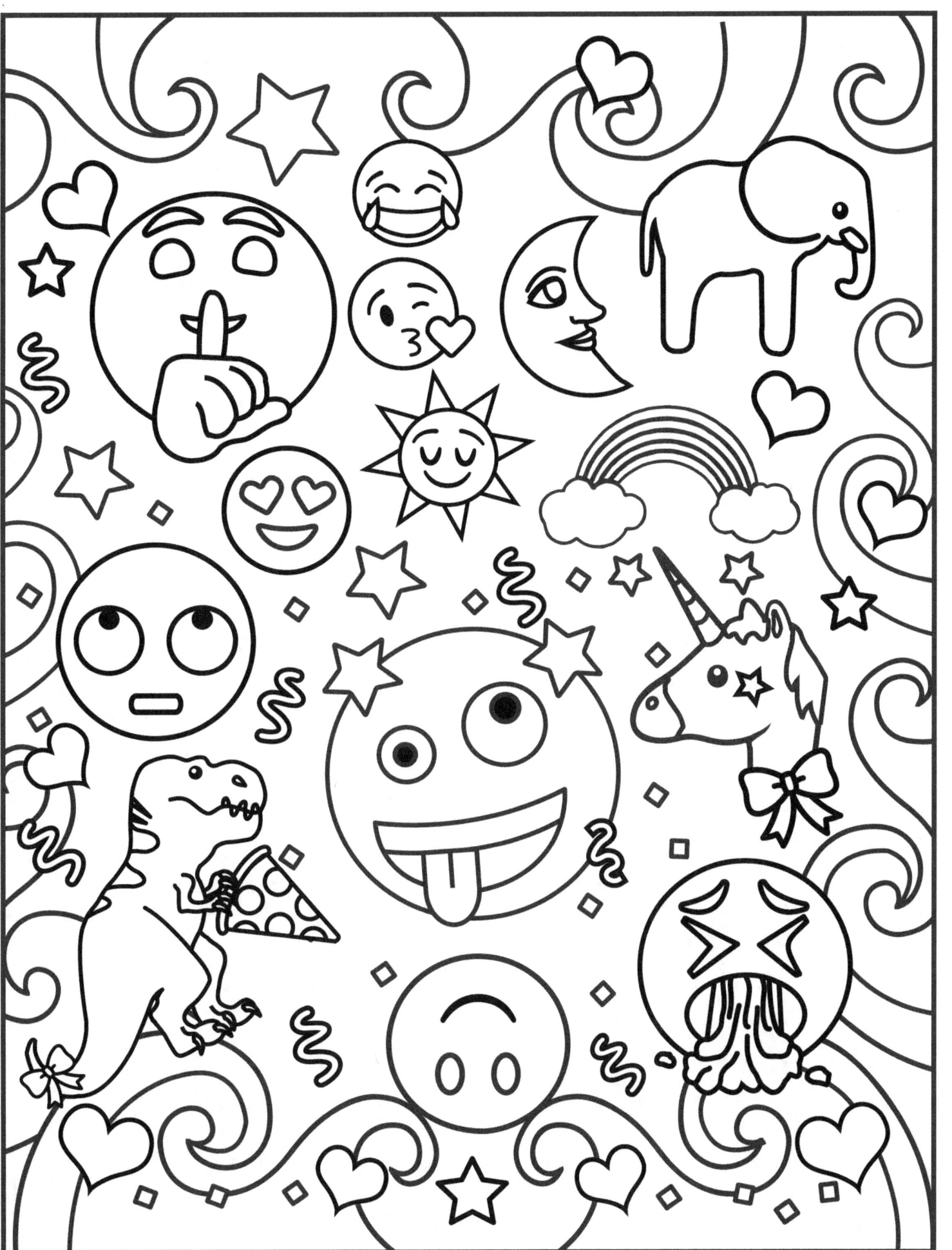

THIS PAGE IS RESERVED FOR
UNICORNS TO COLOR ONLY

VIOLATORS WILL BE TURNED INTO RAINBOWS

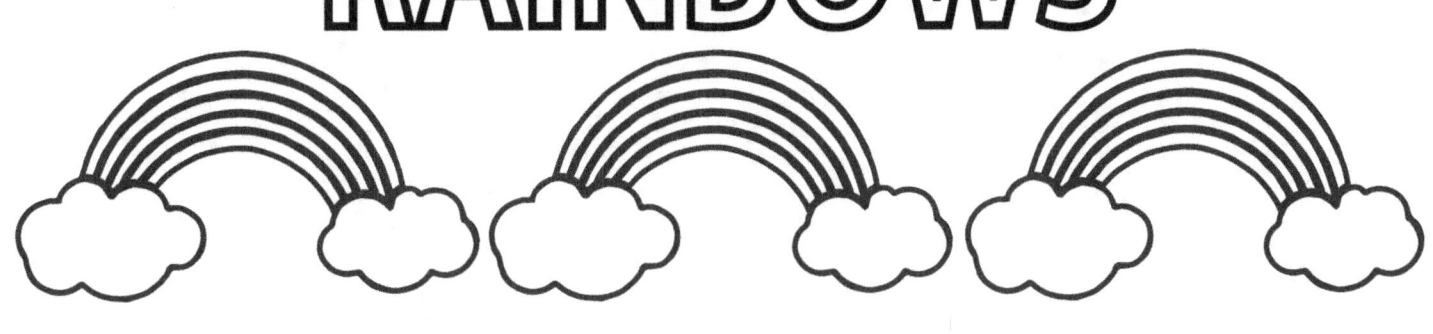

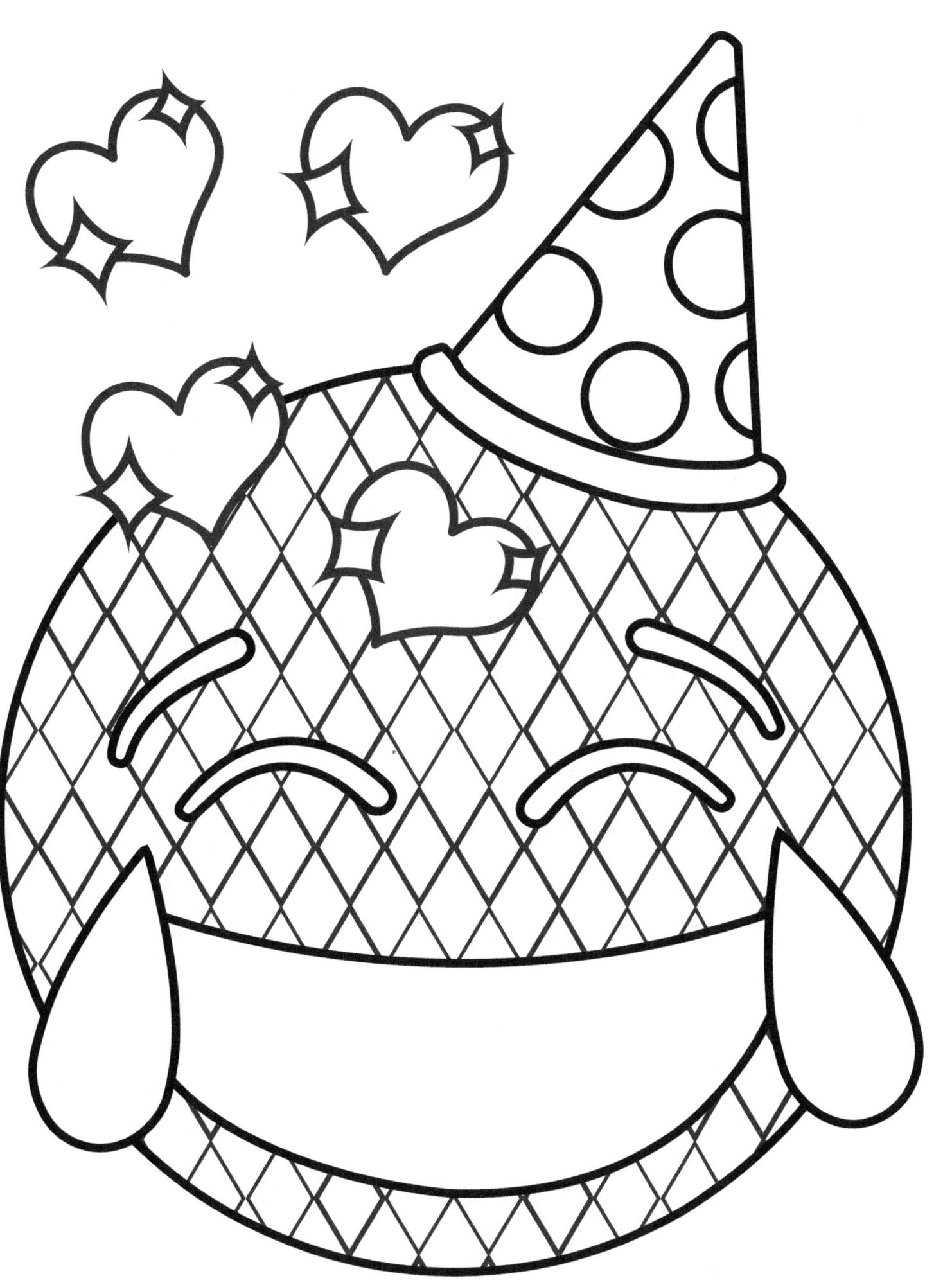

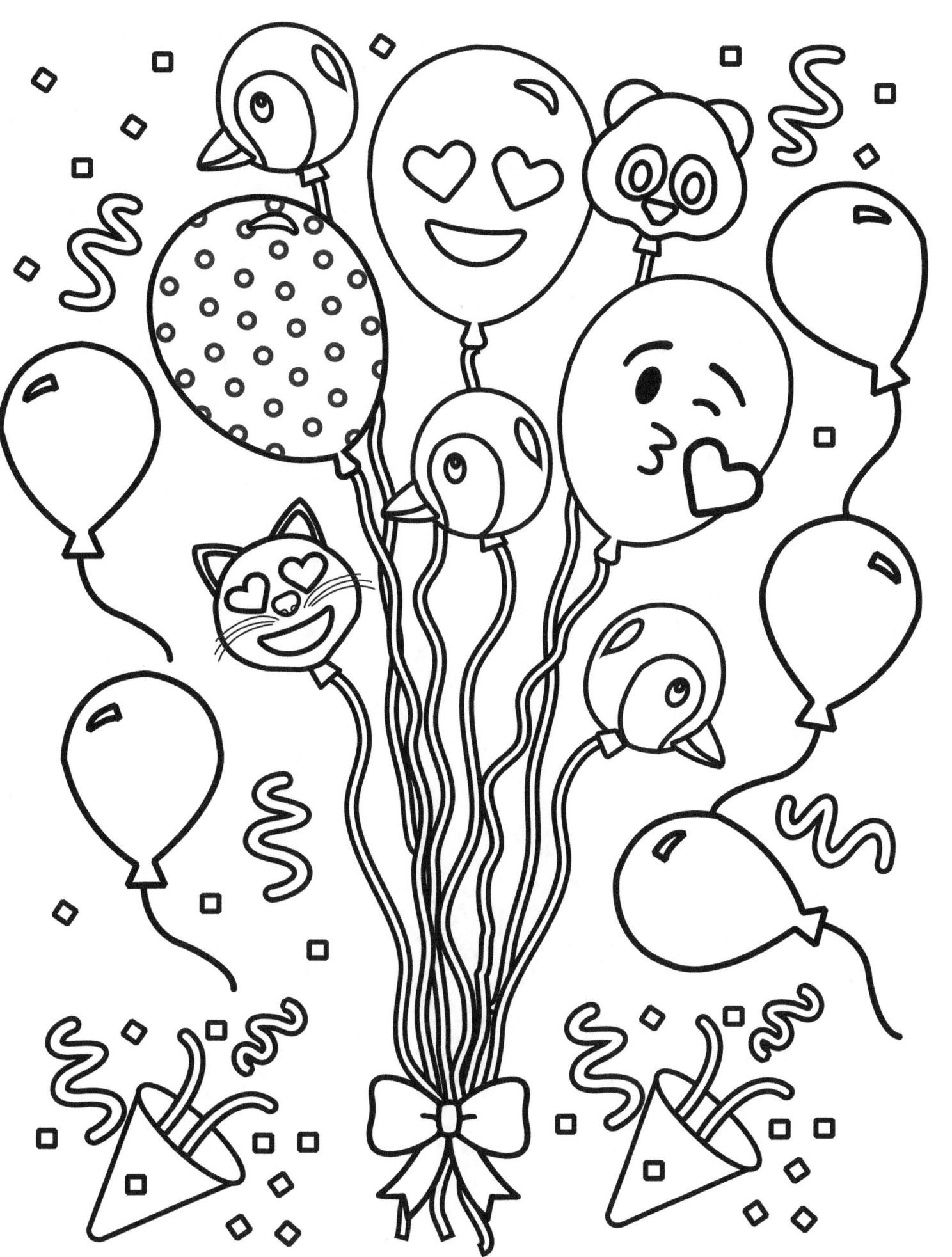

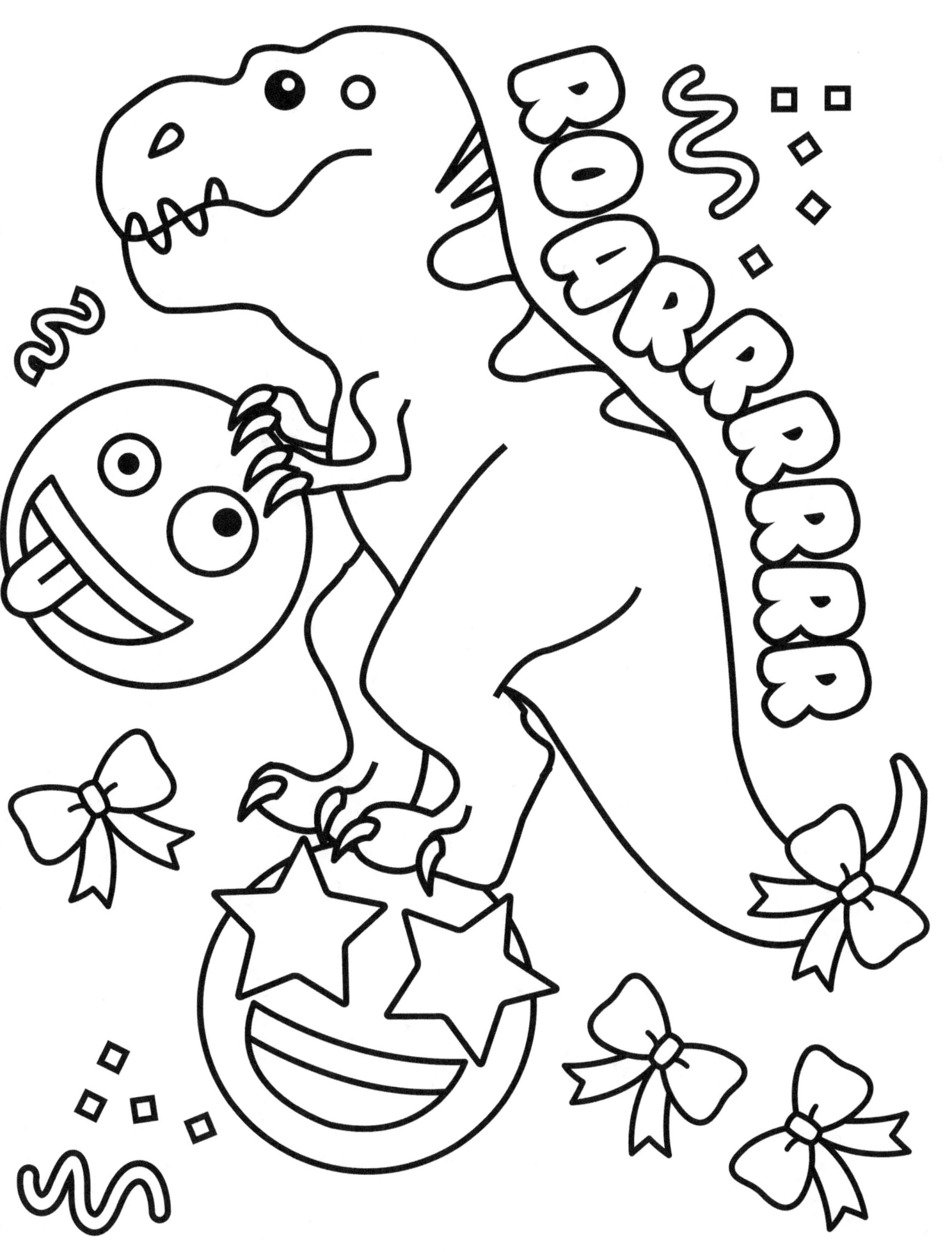

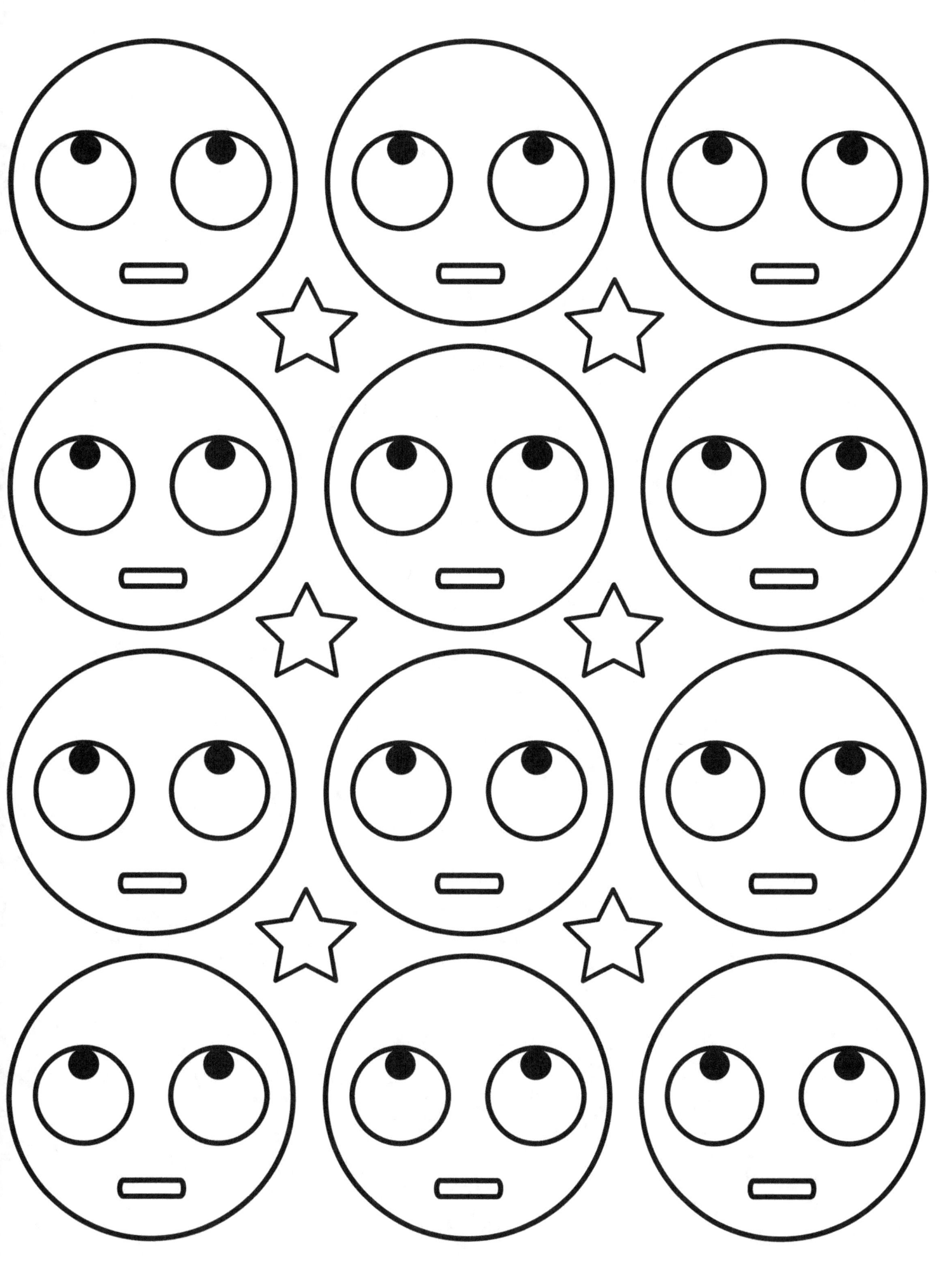

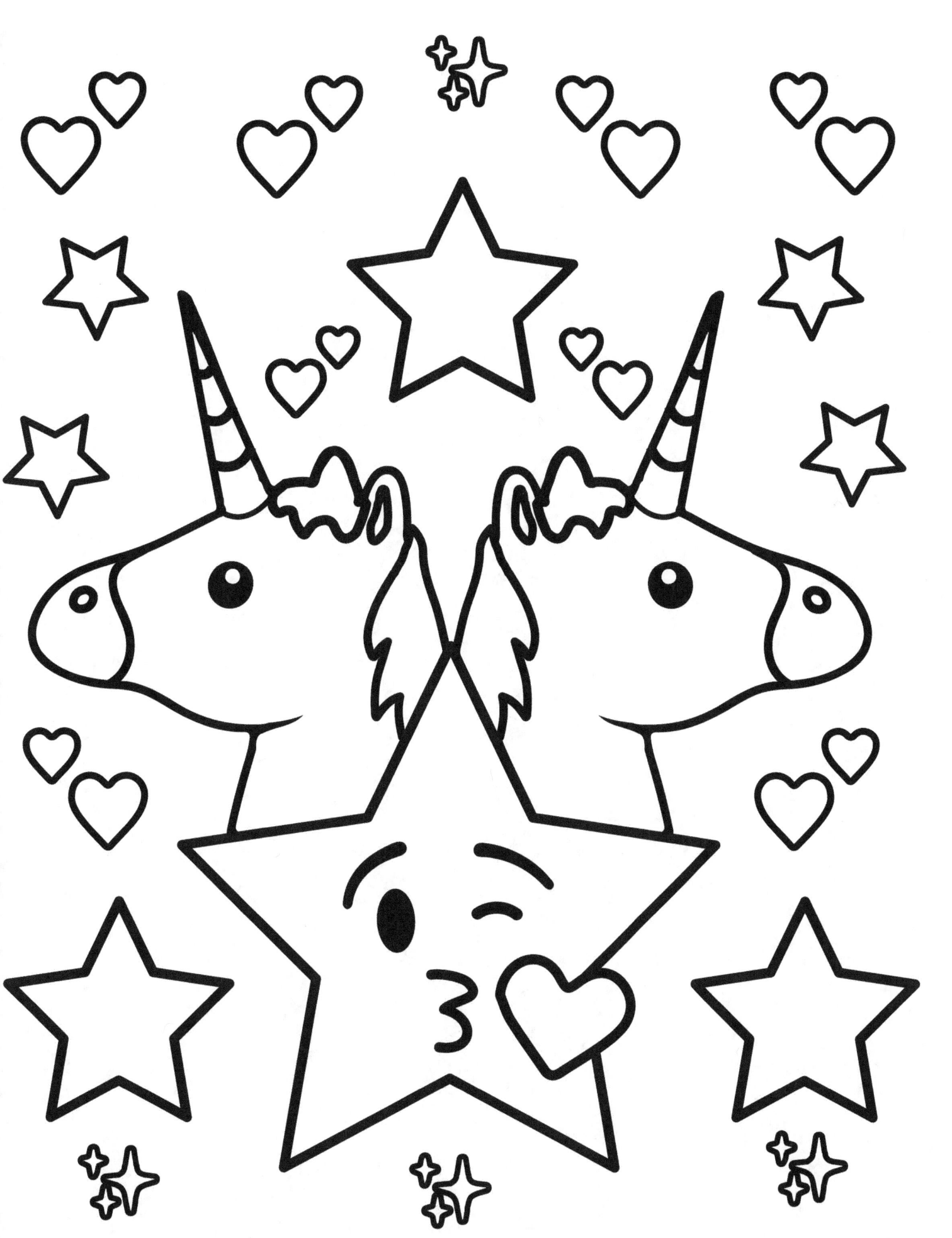

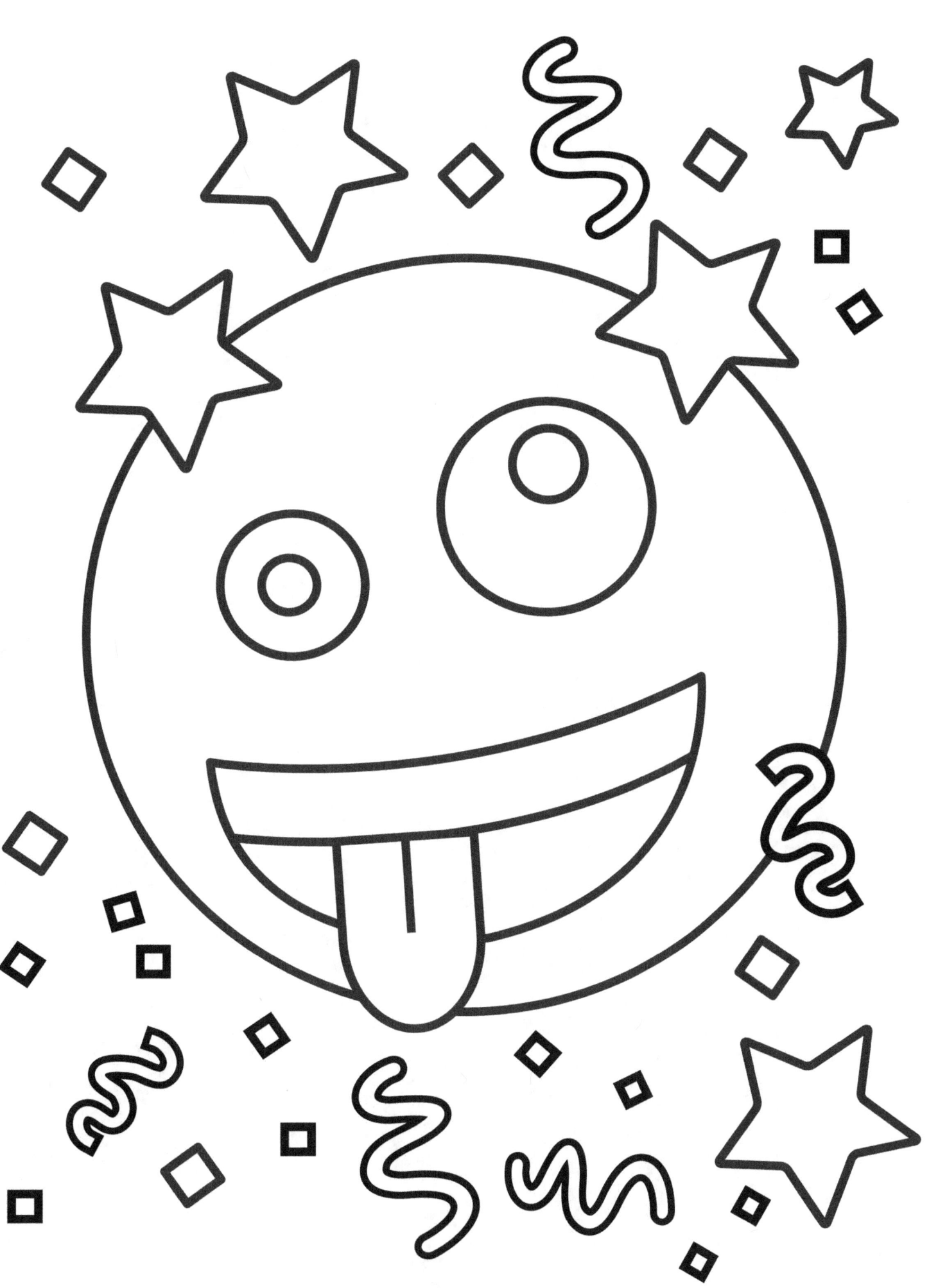

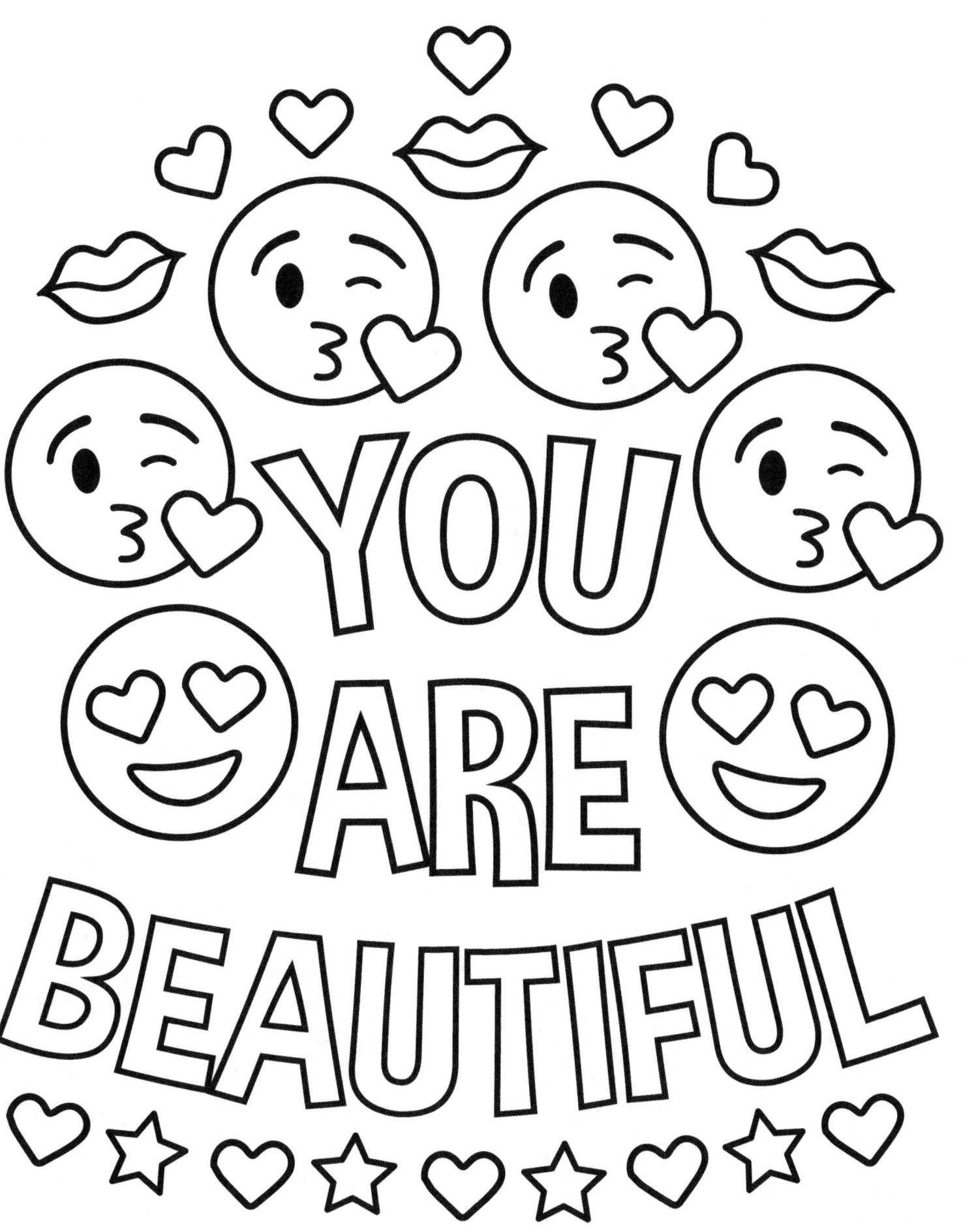

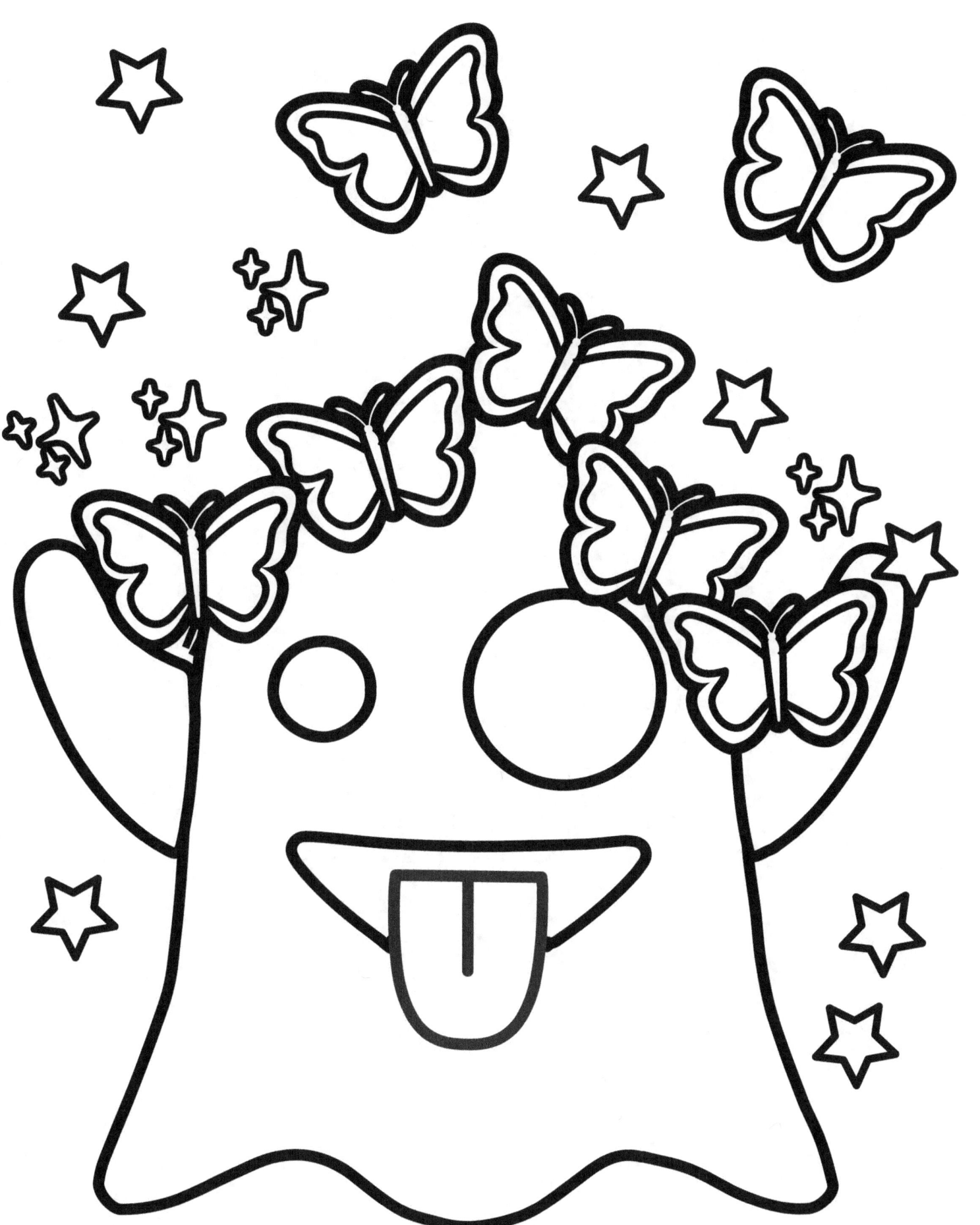

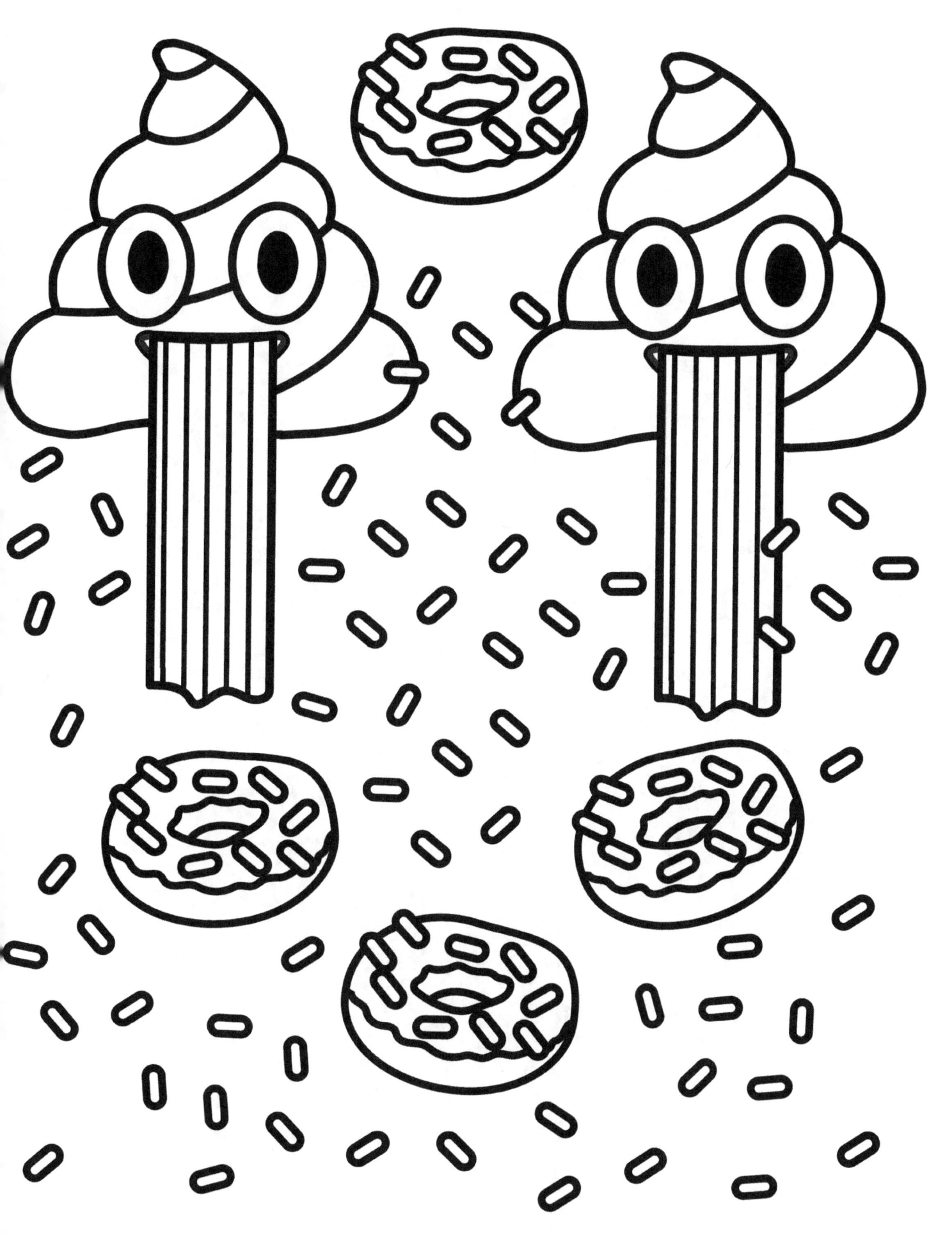

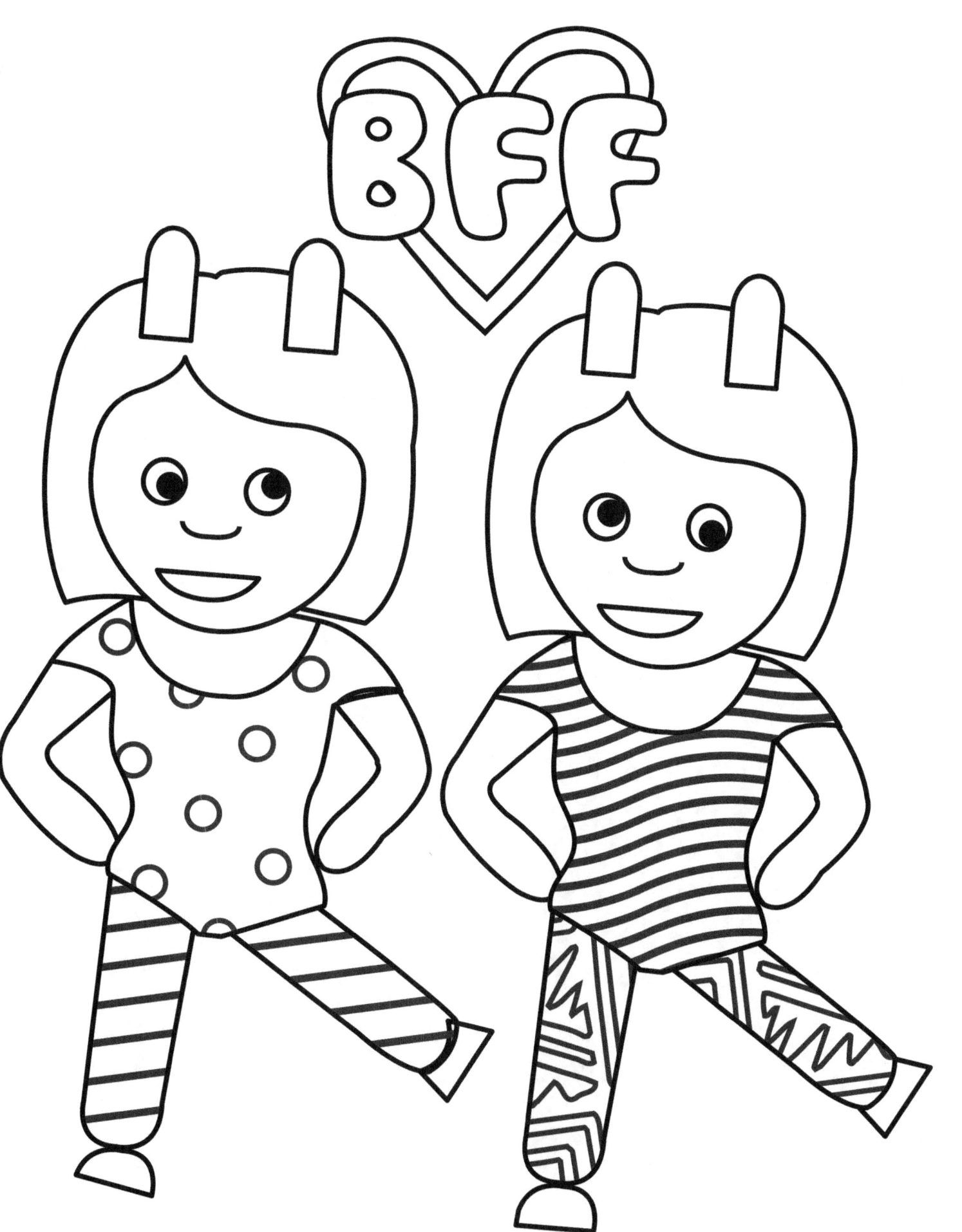

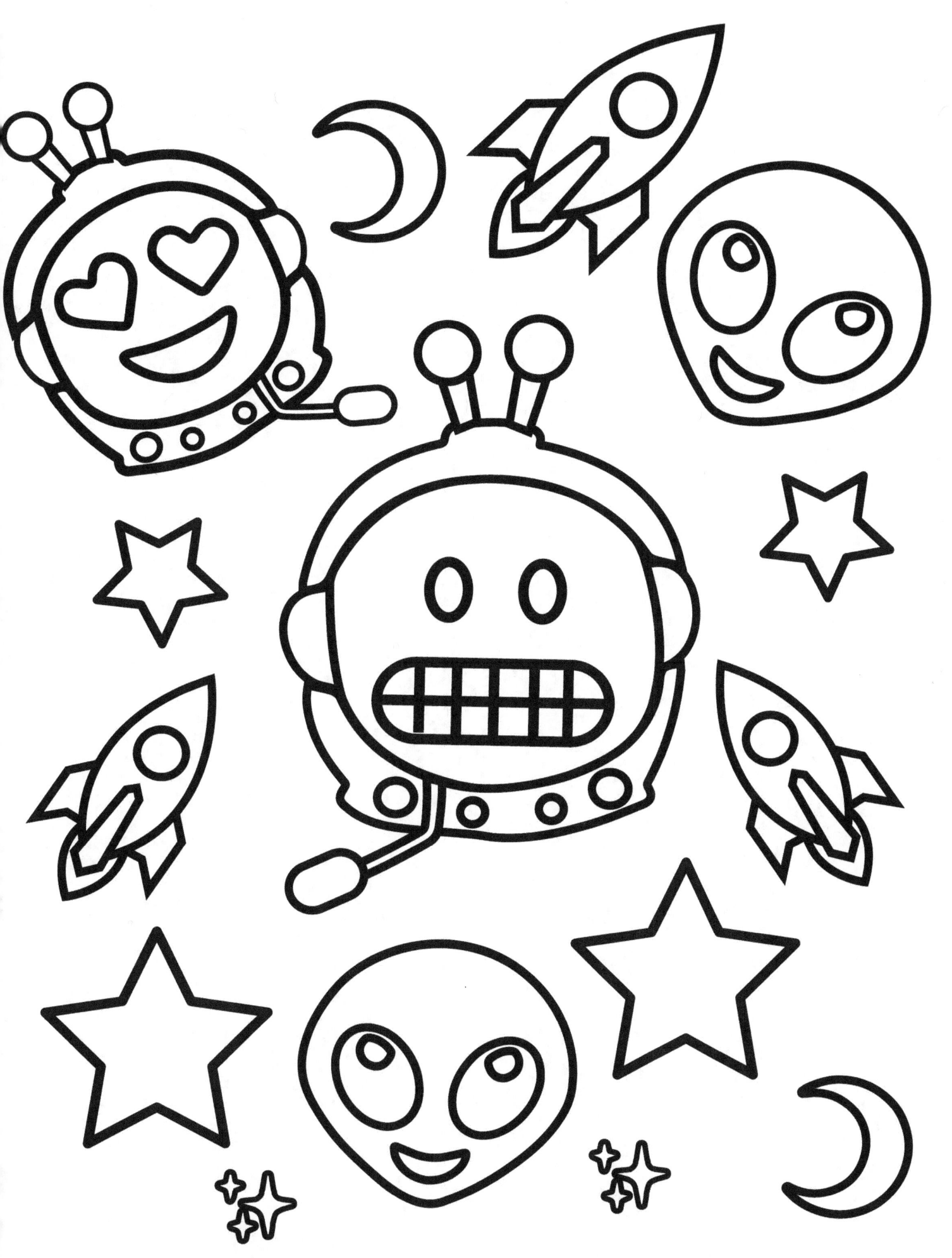

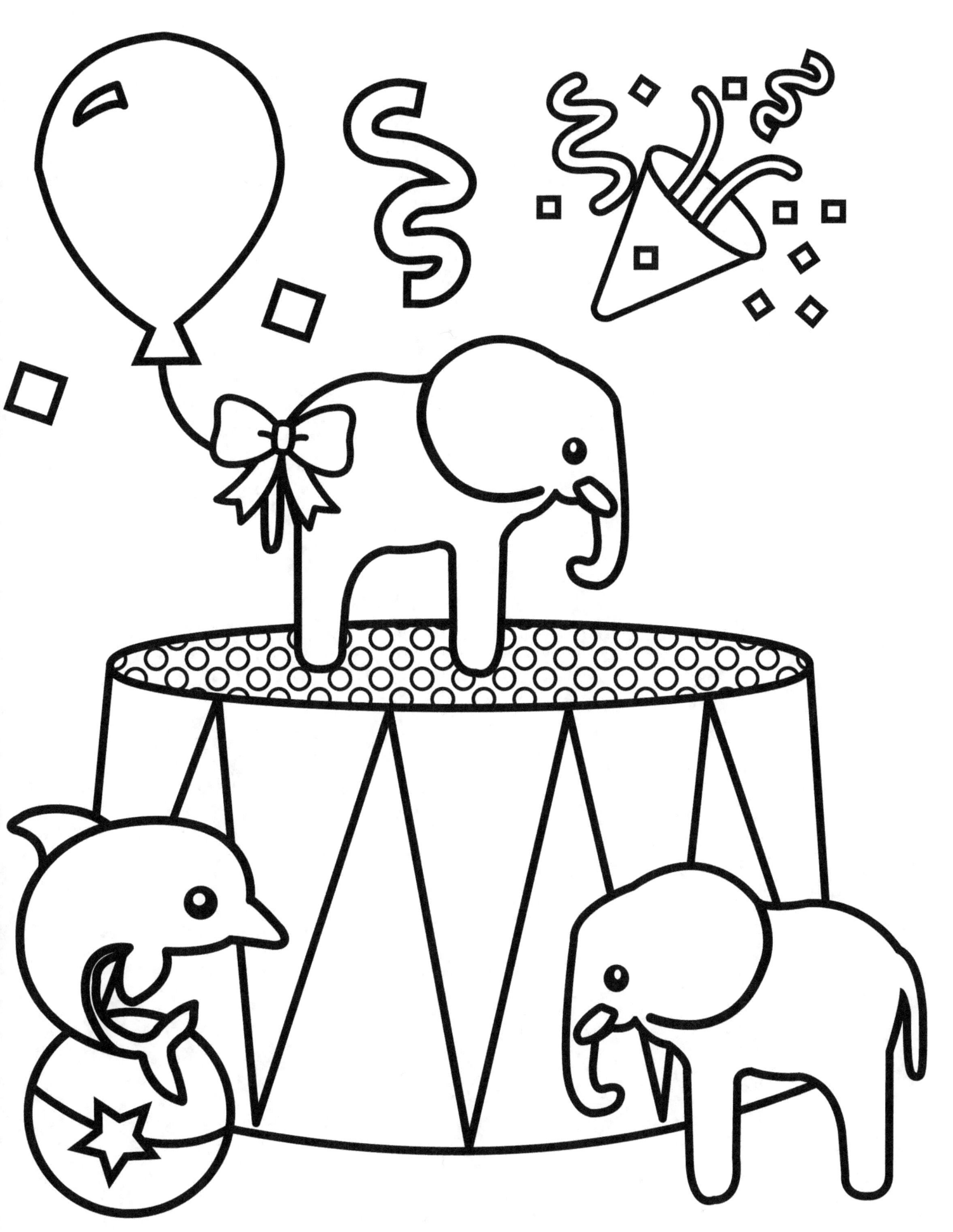

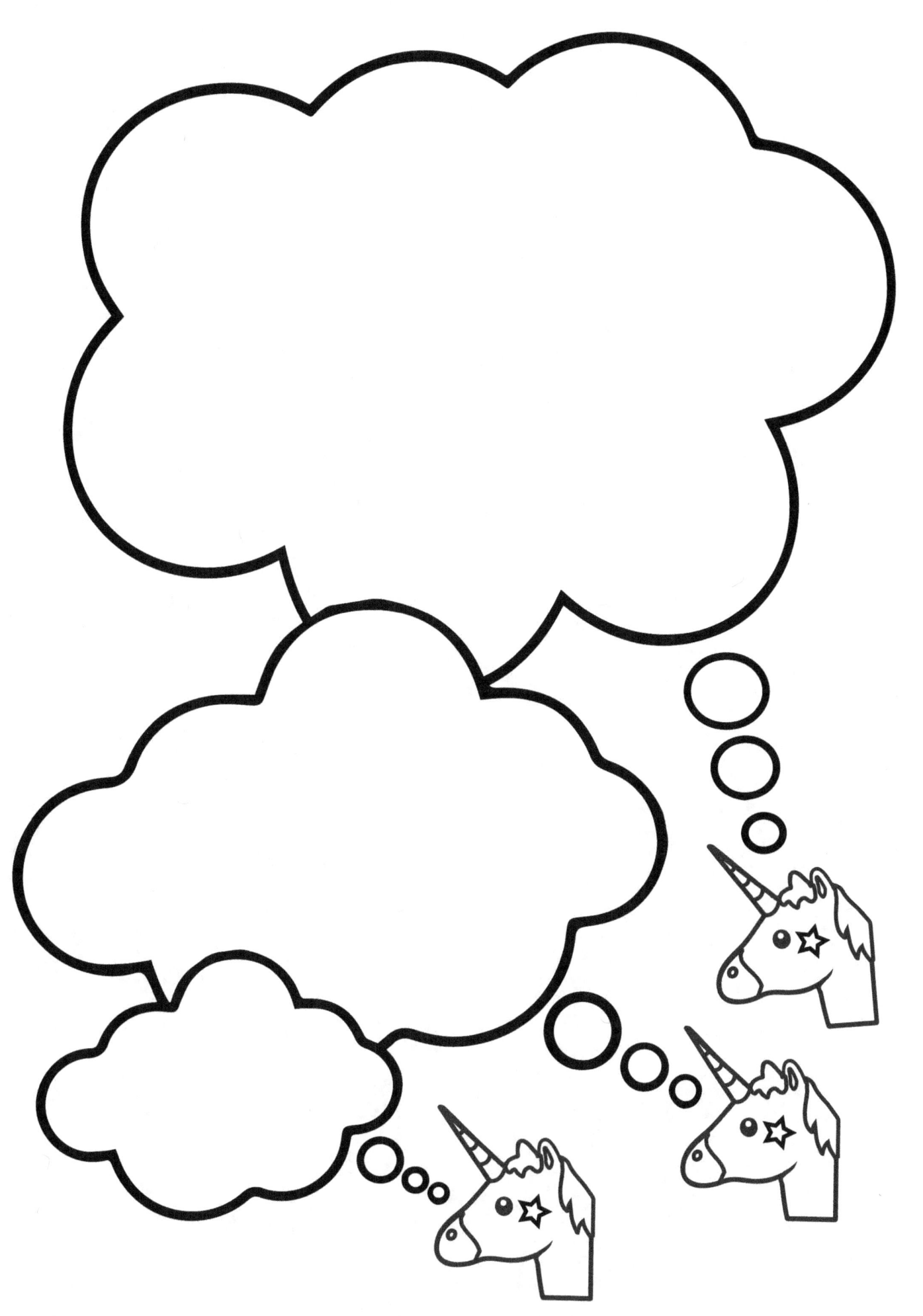

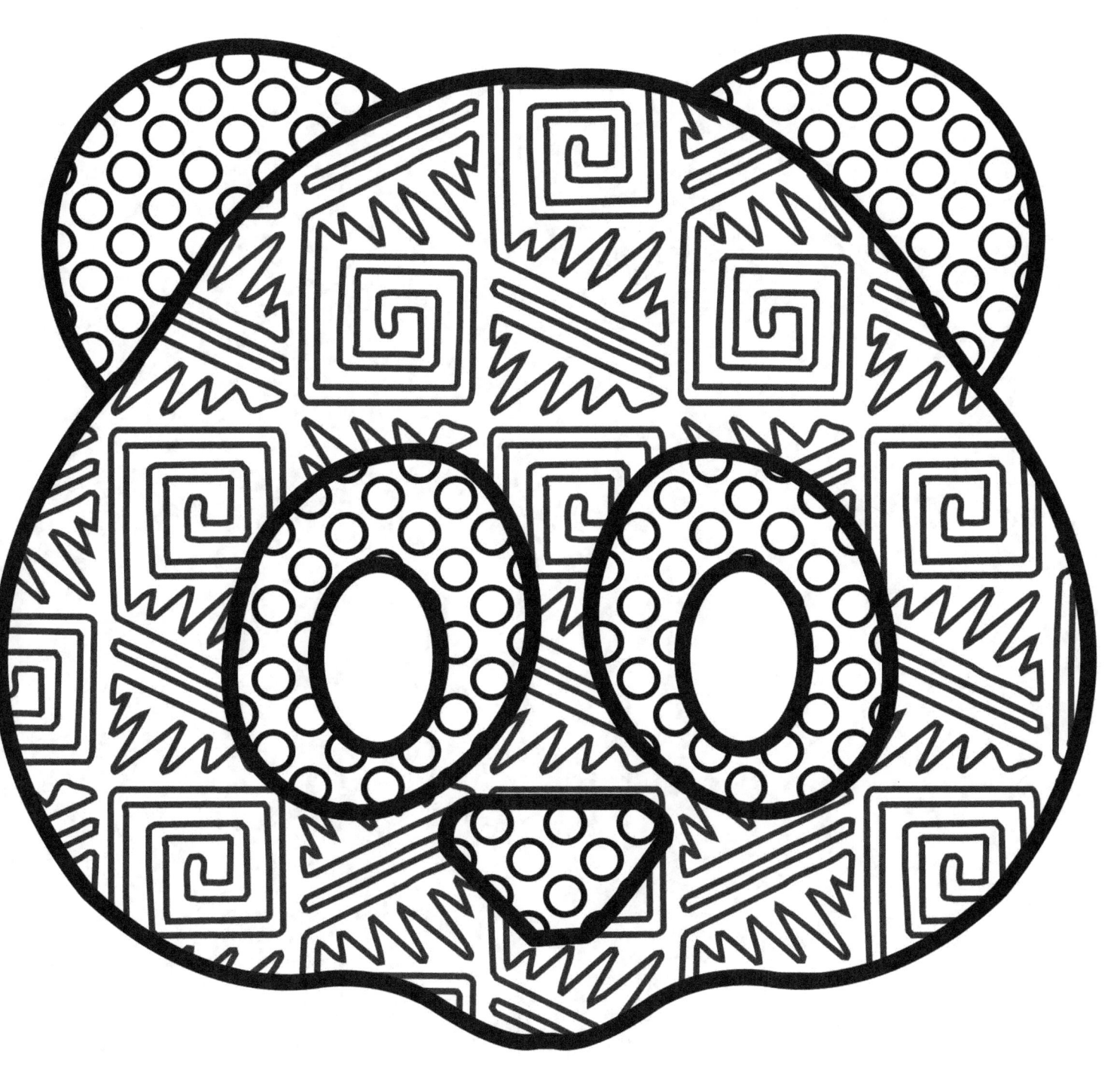

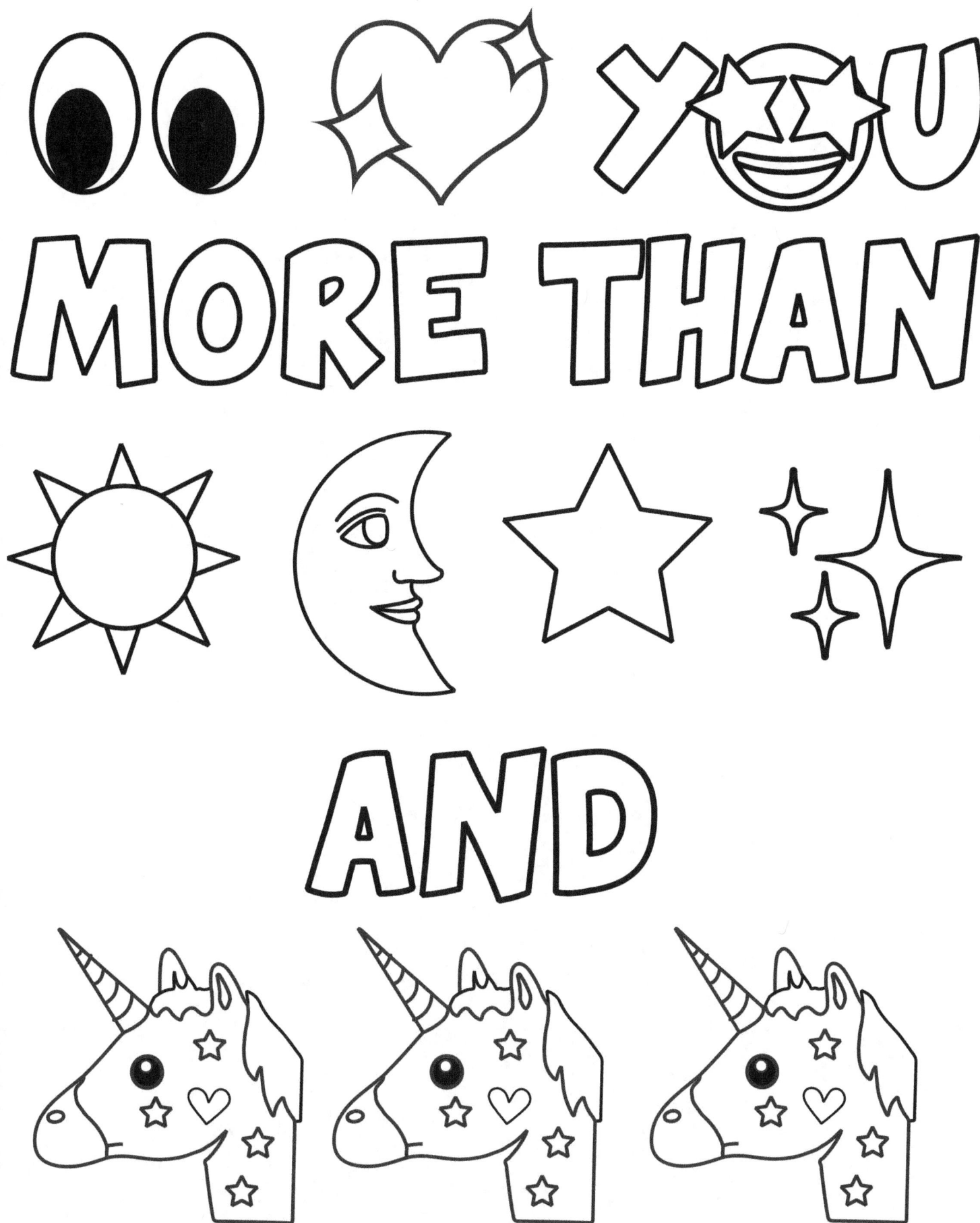

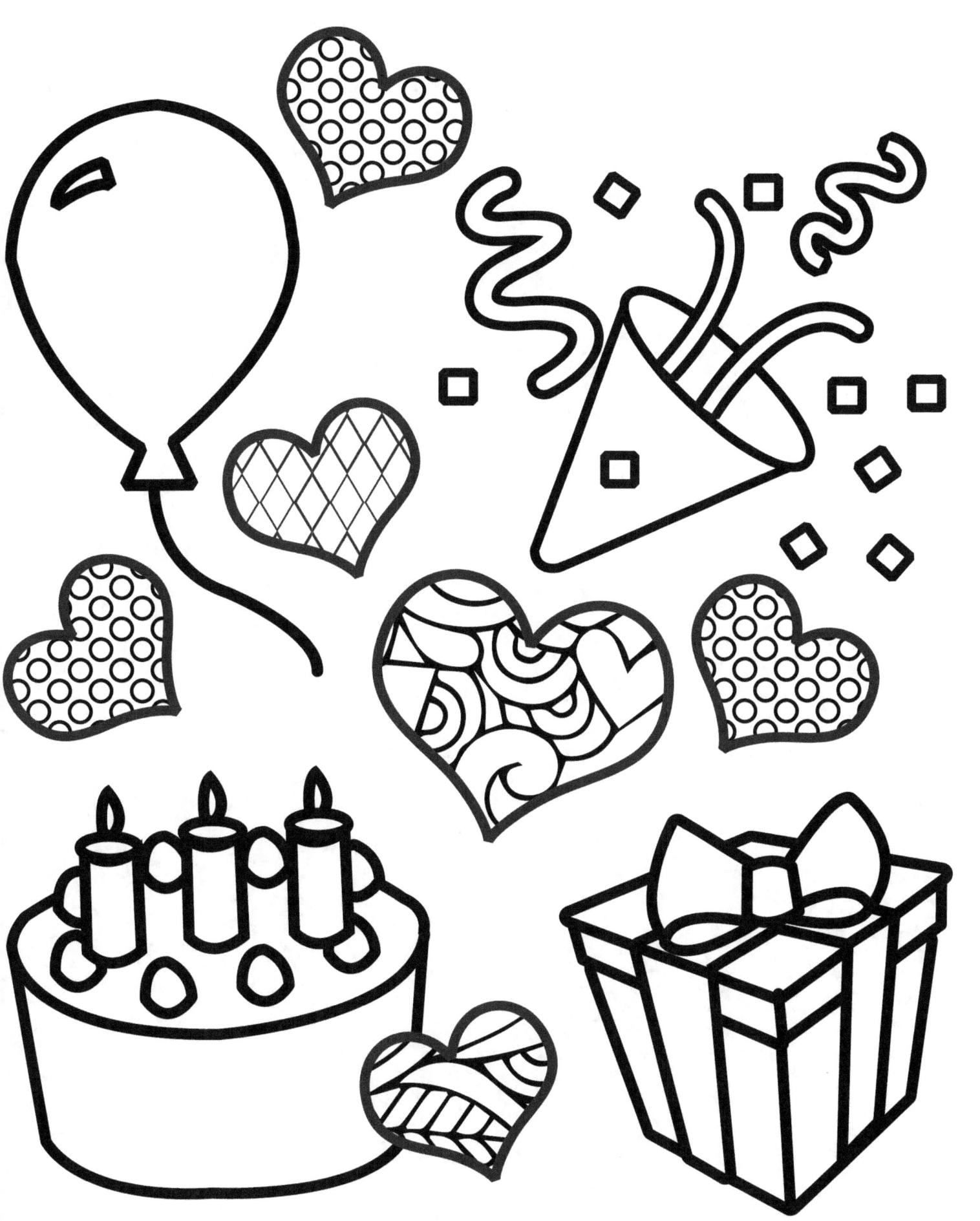

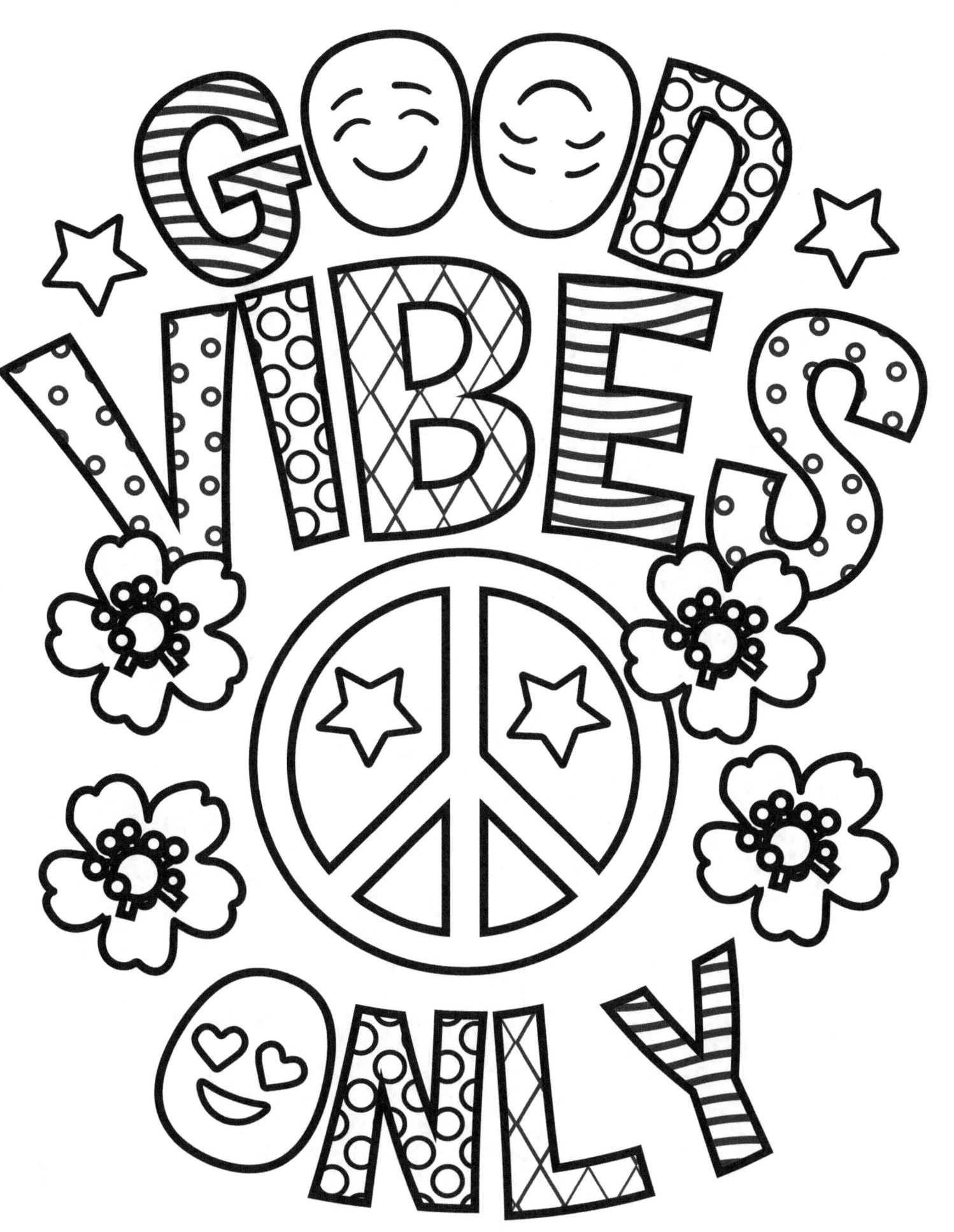

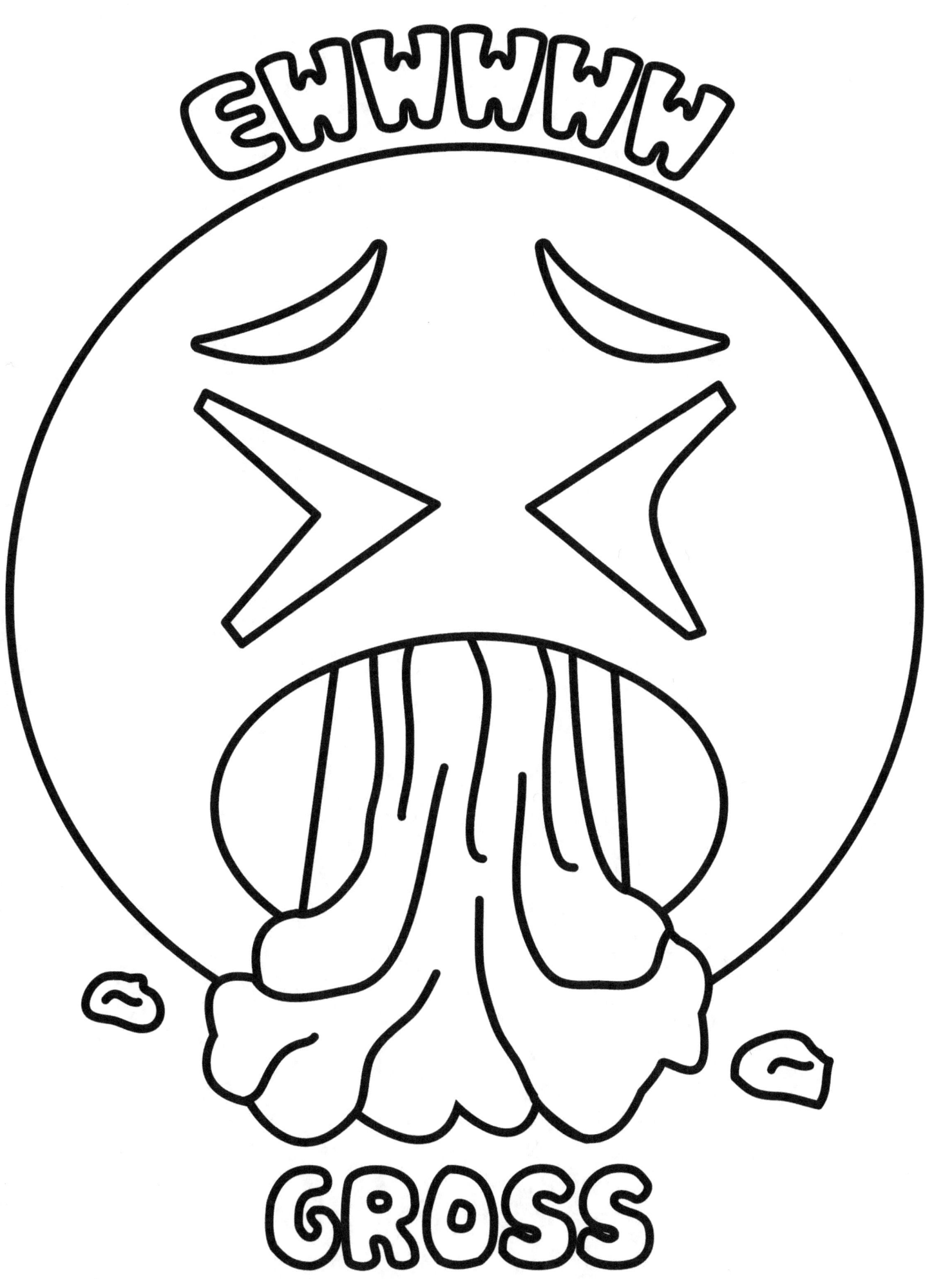

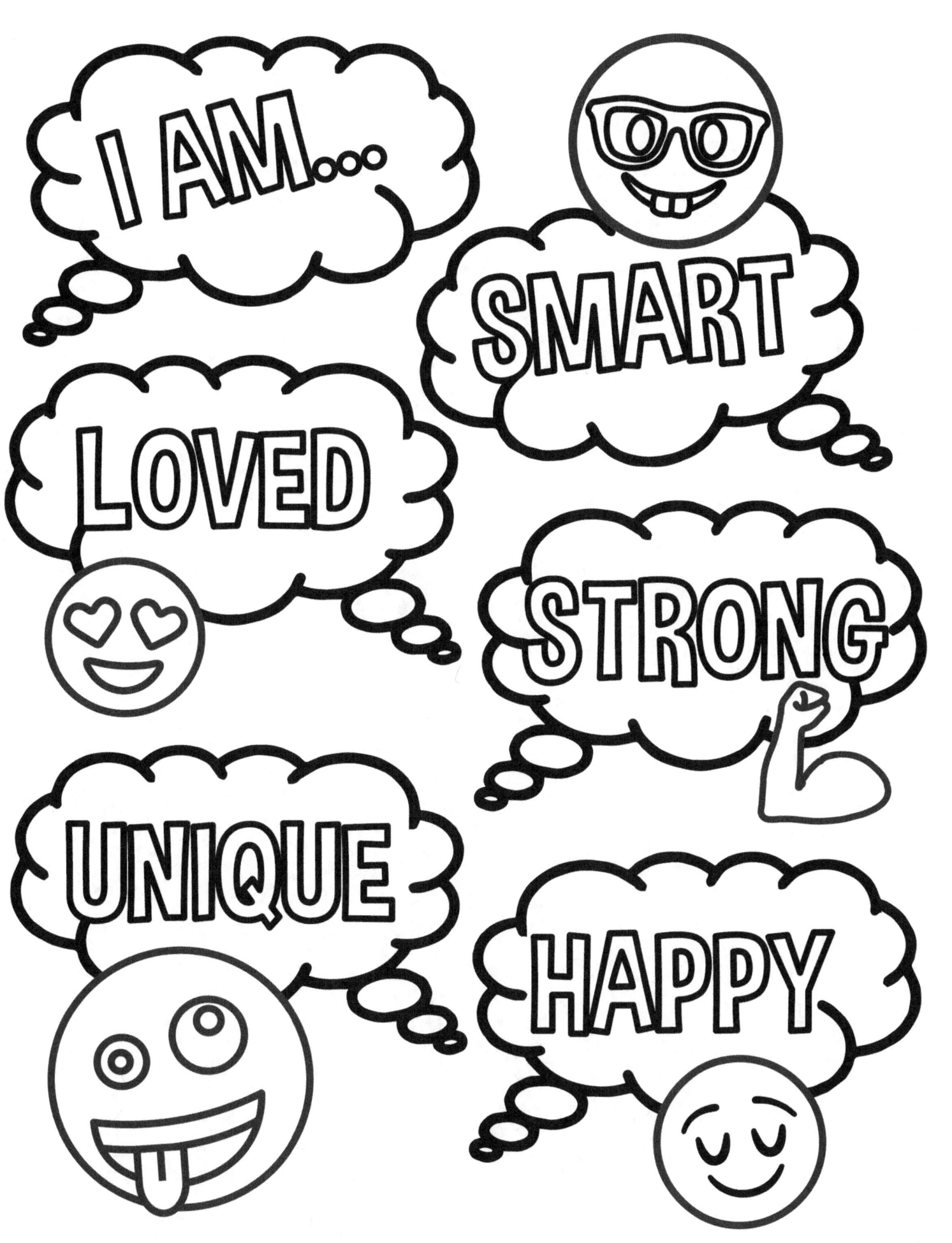

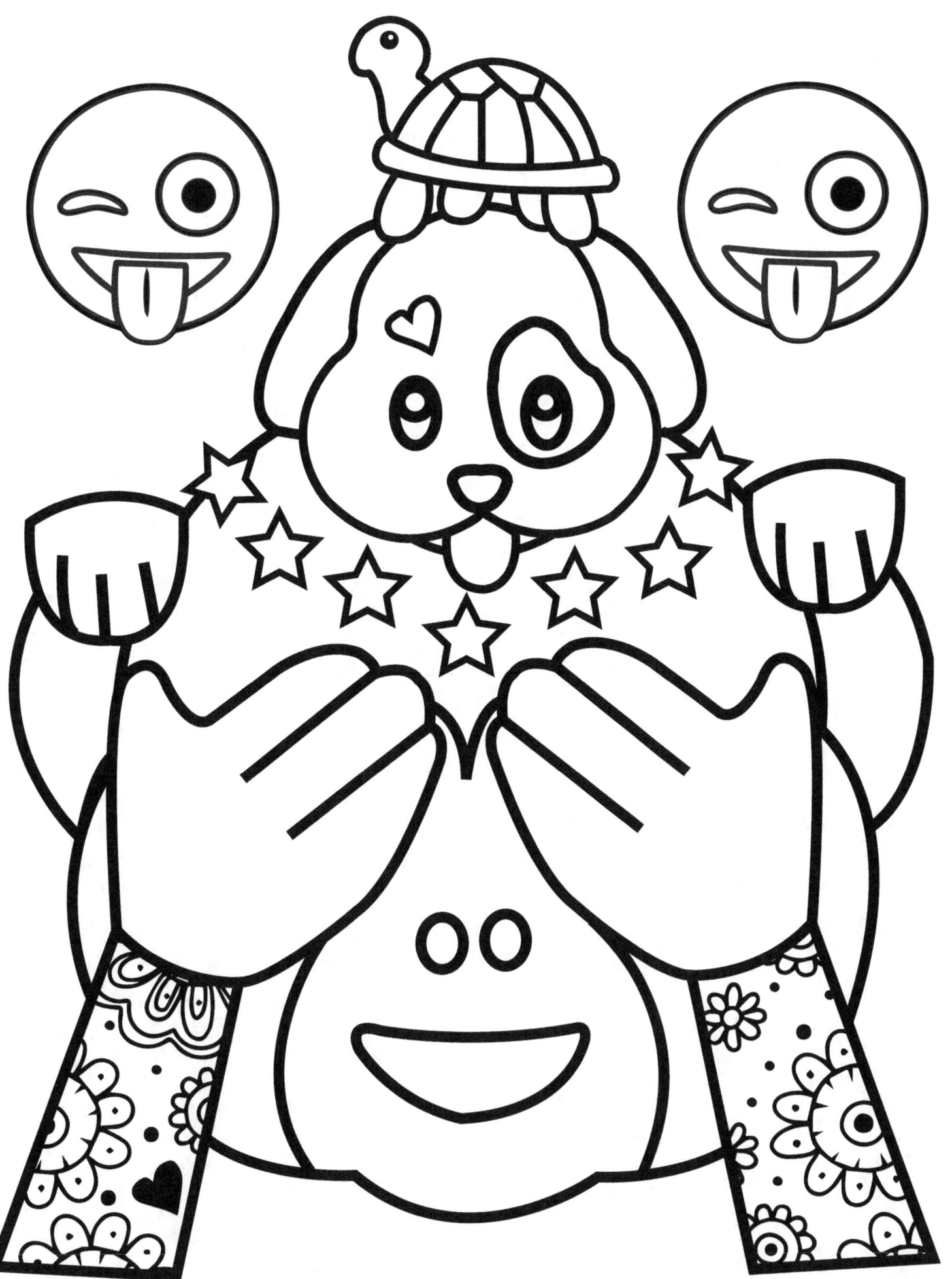

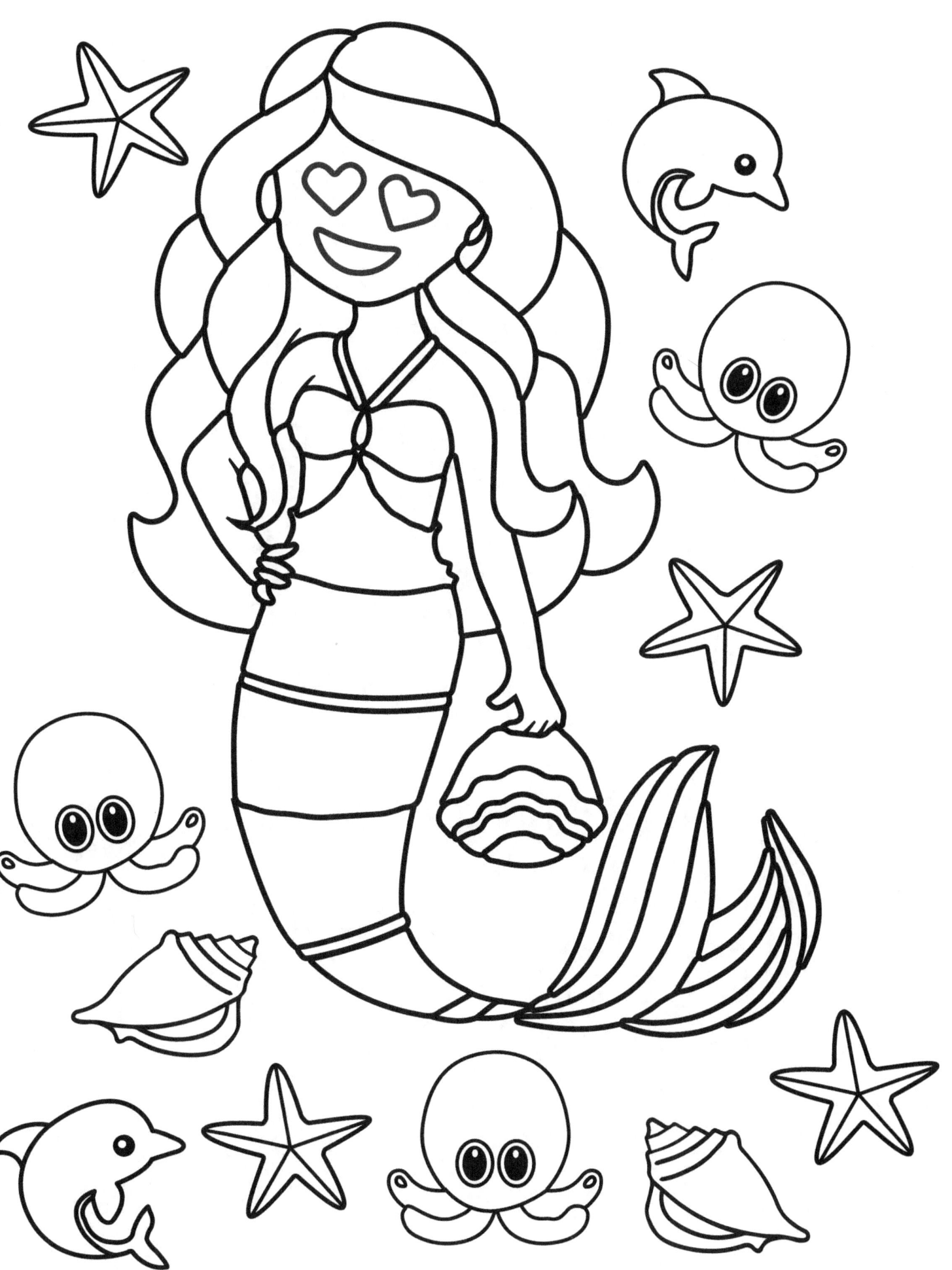

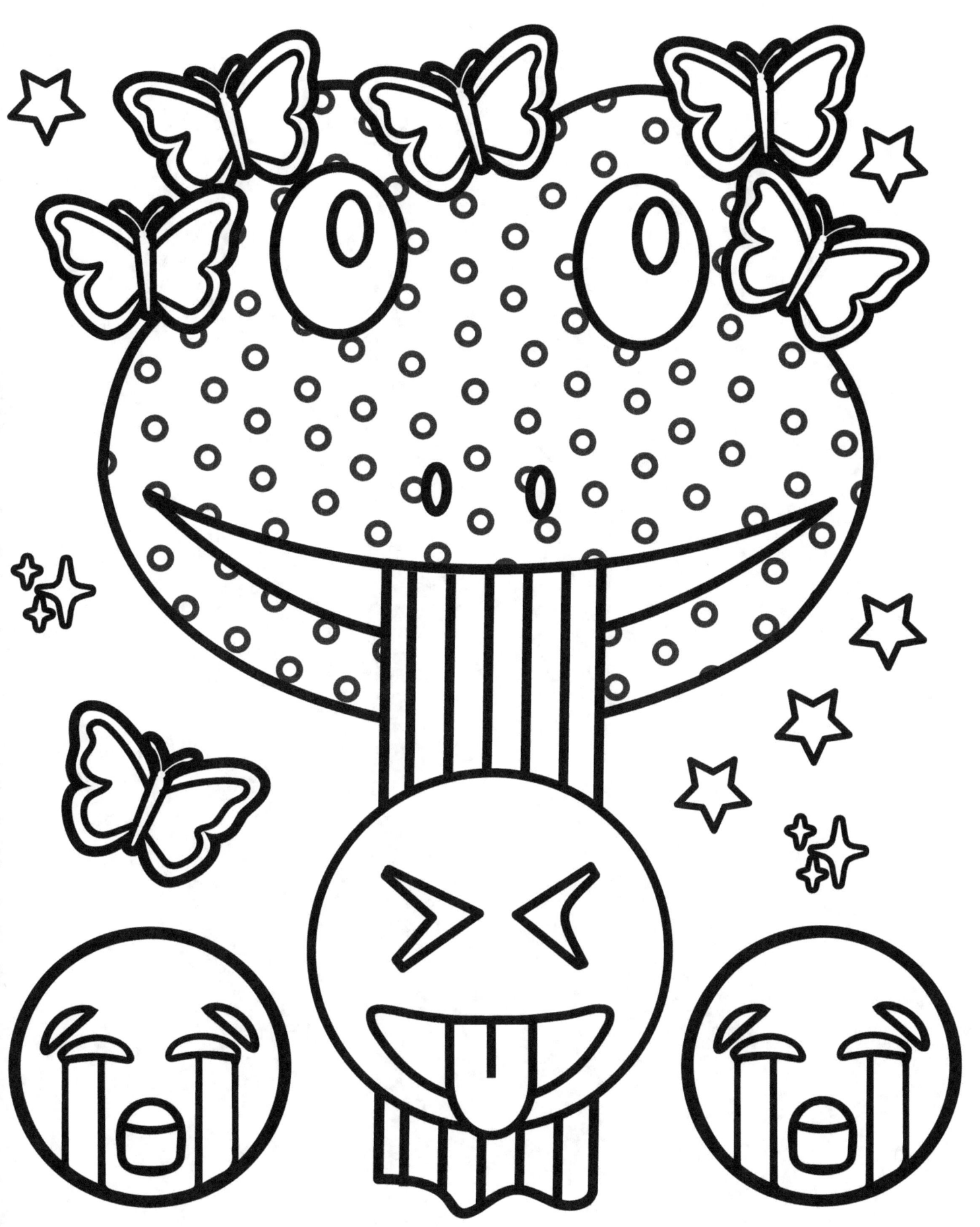

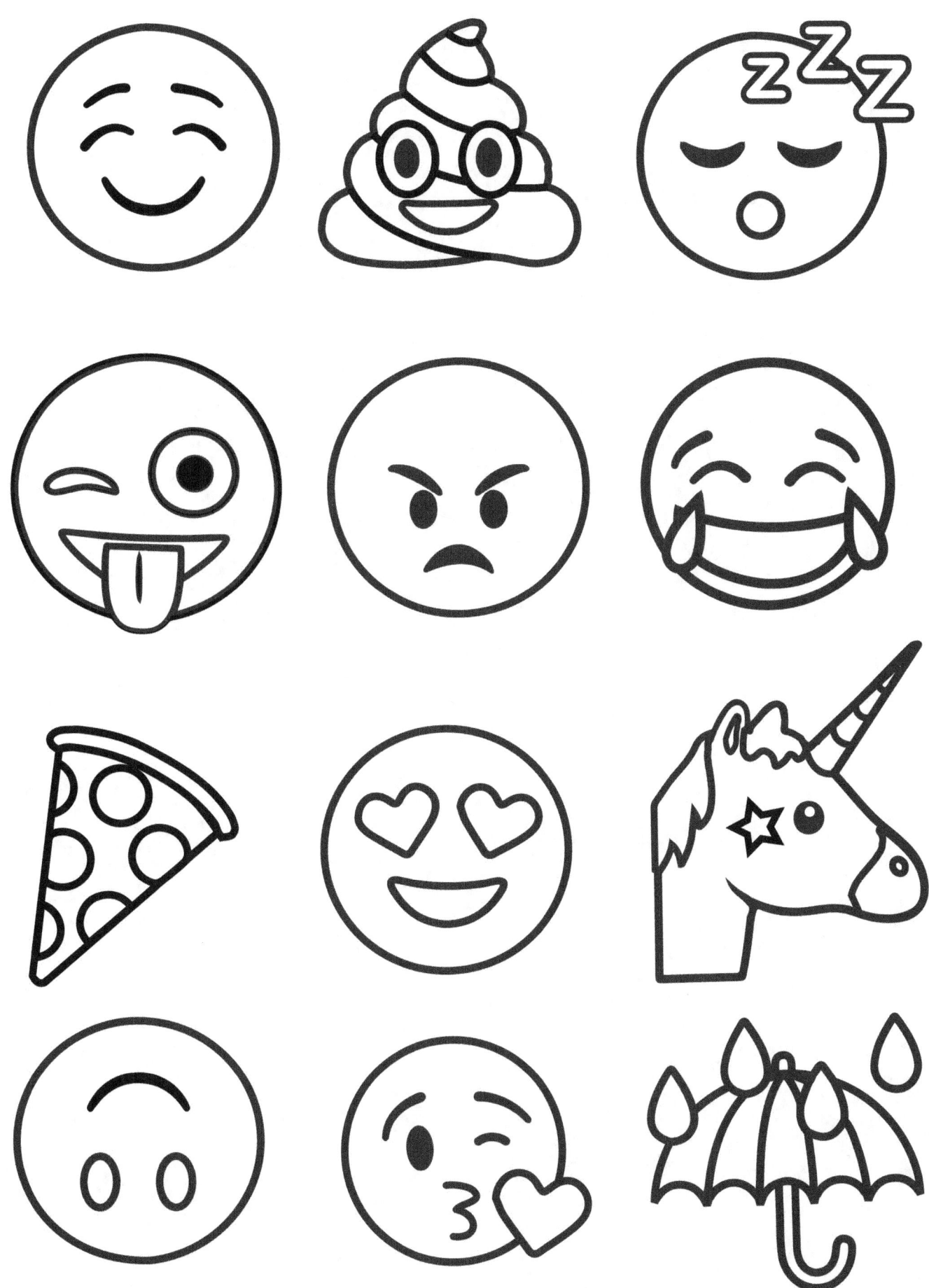

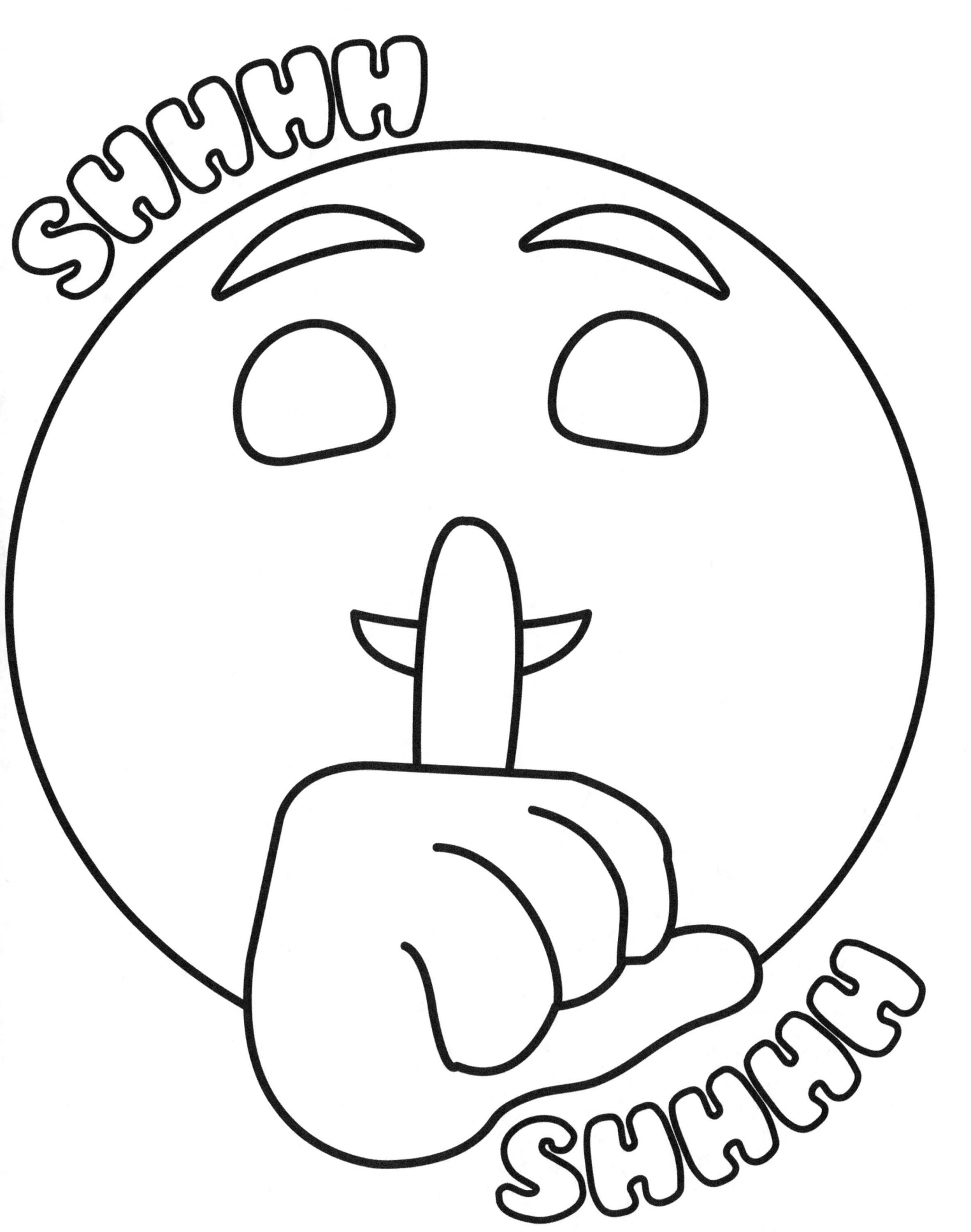

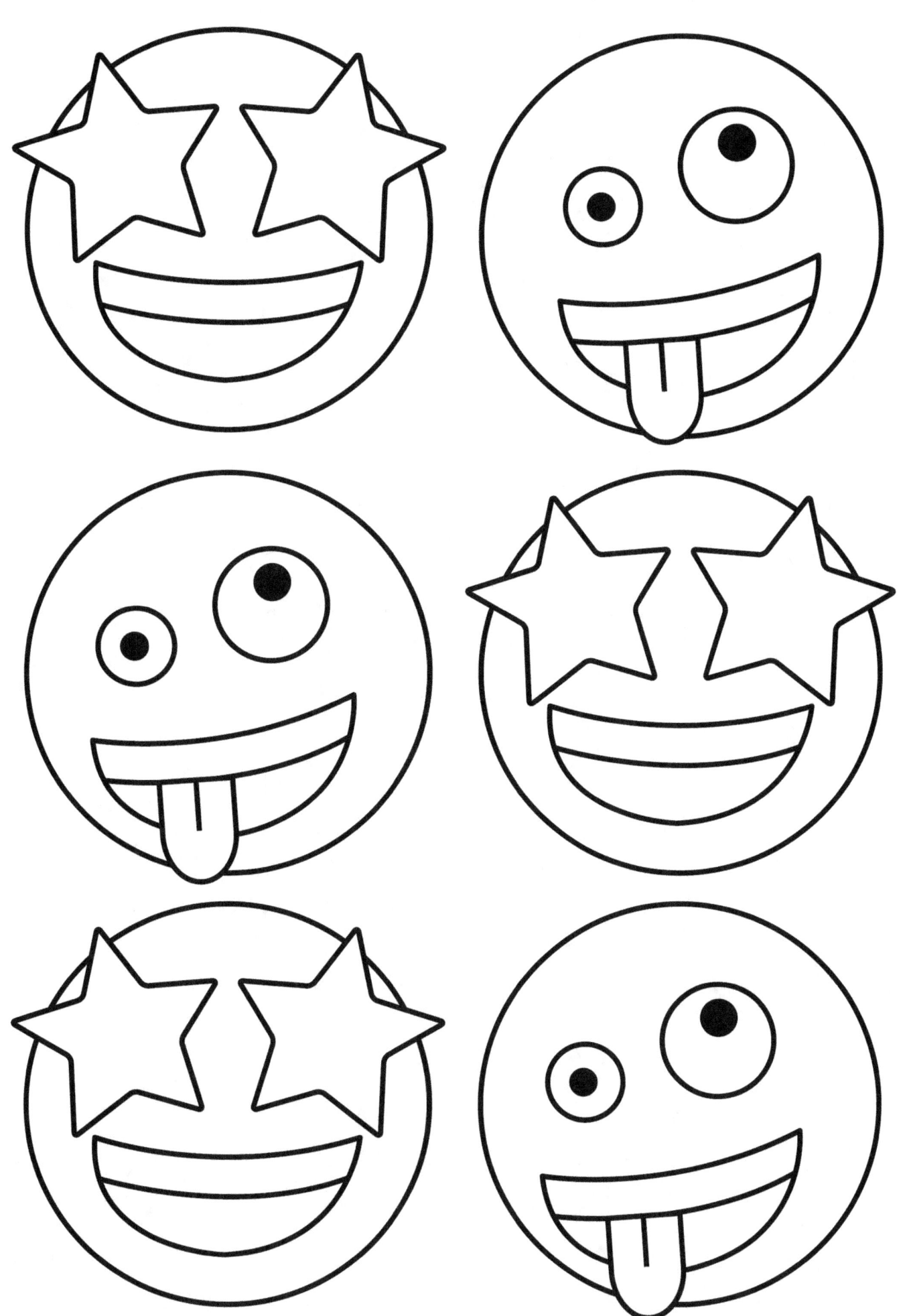

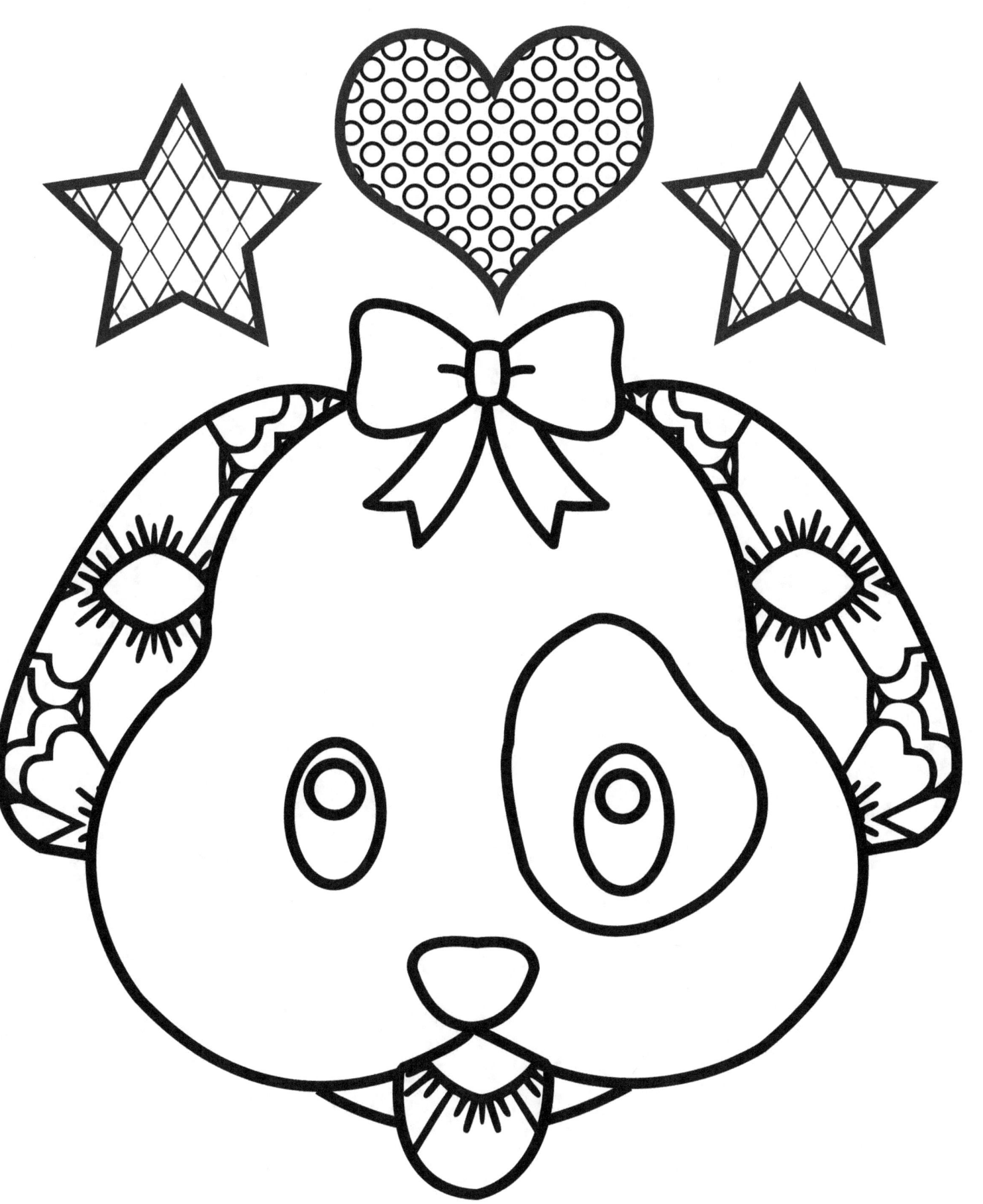

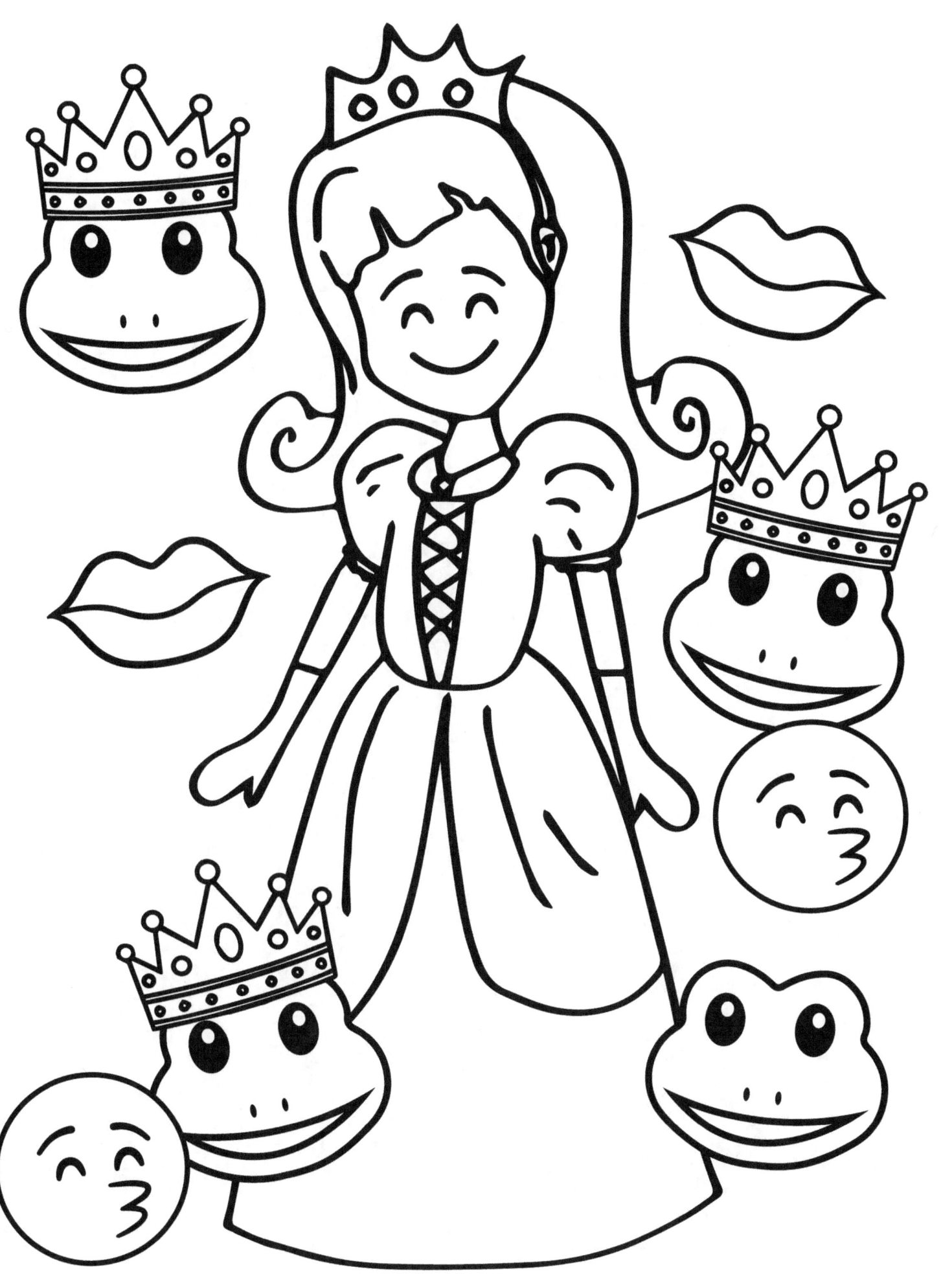

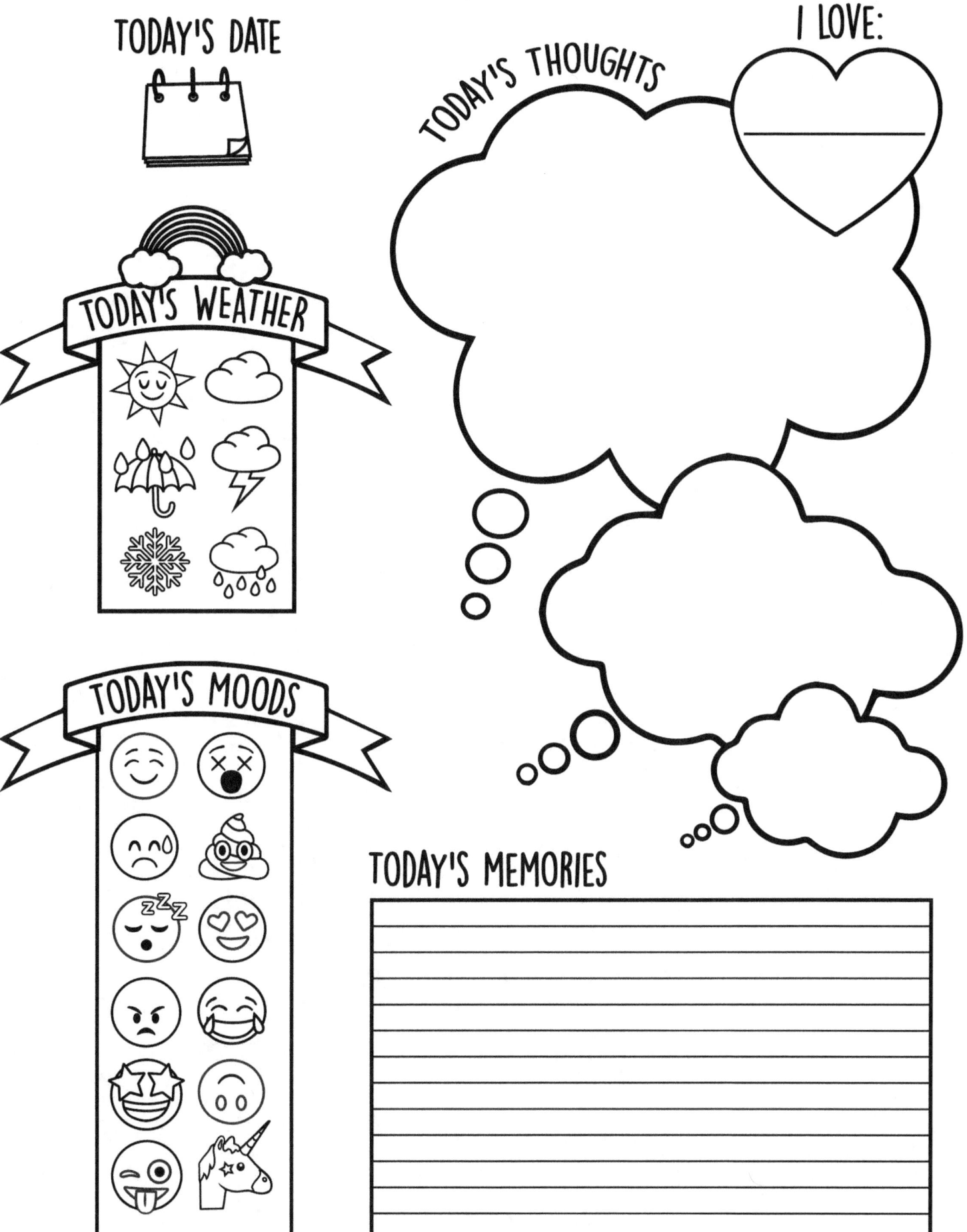

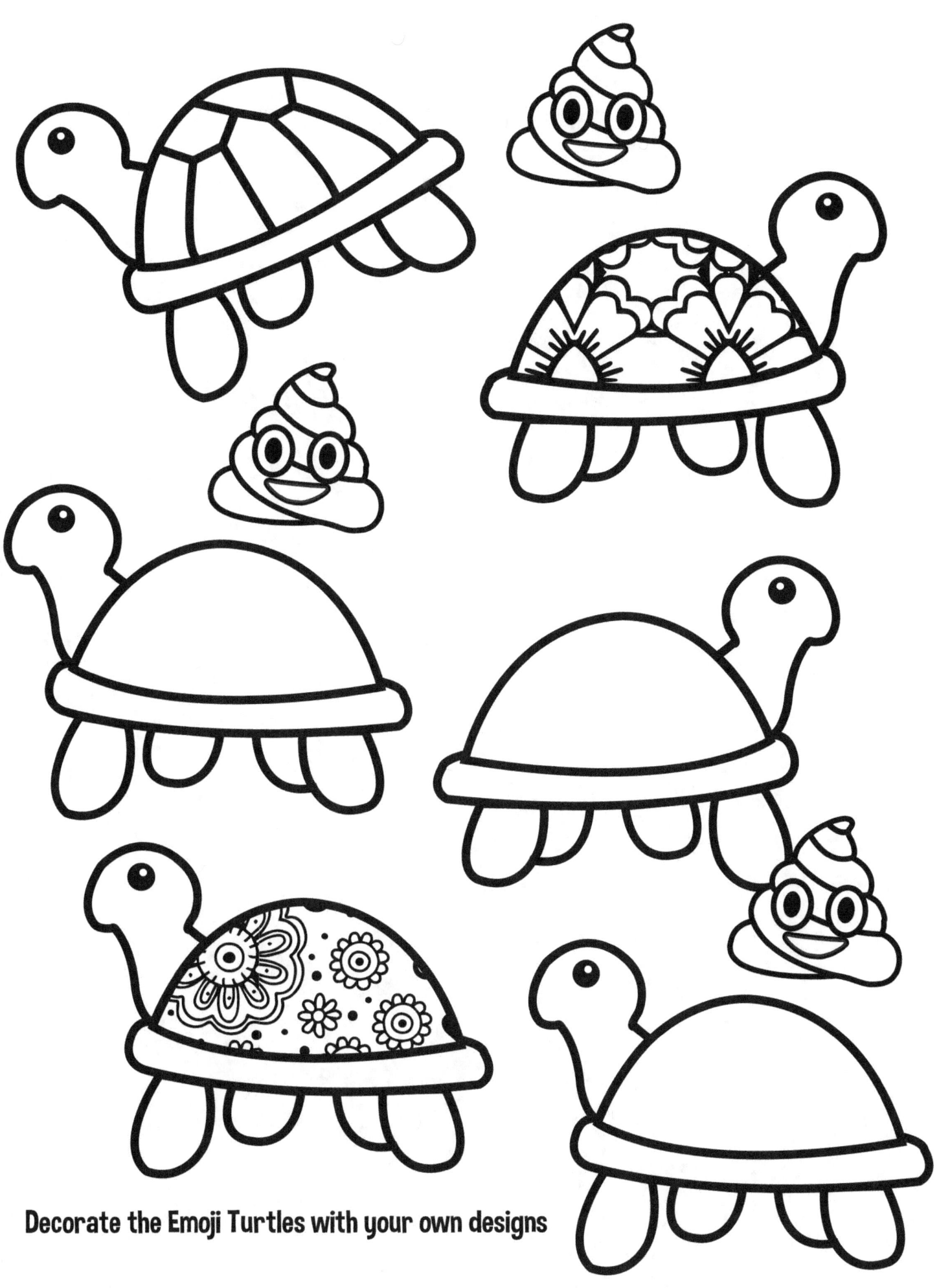

Decorate the Emoji Turtles with your own designs

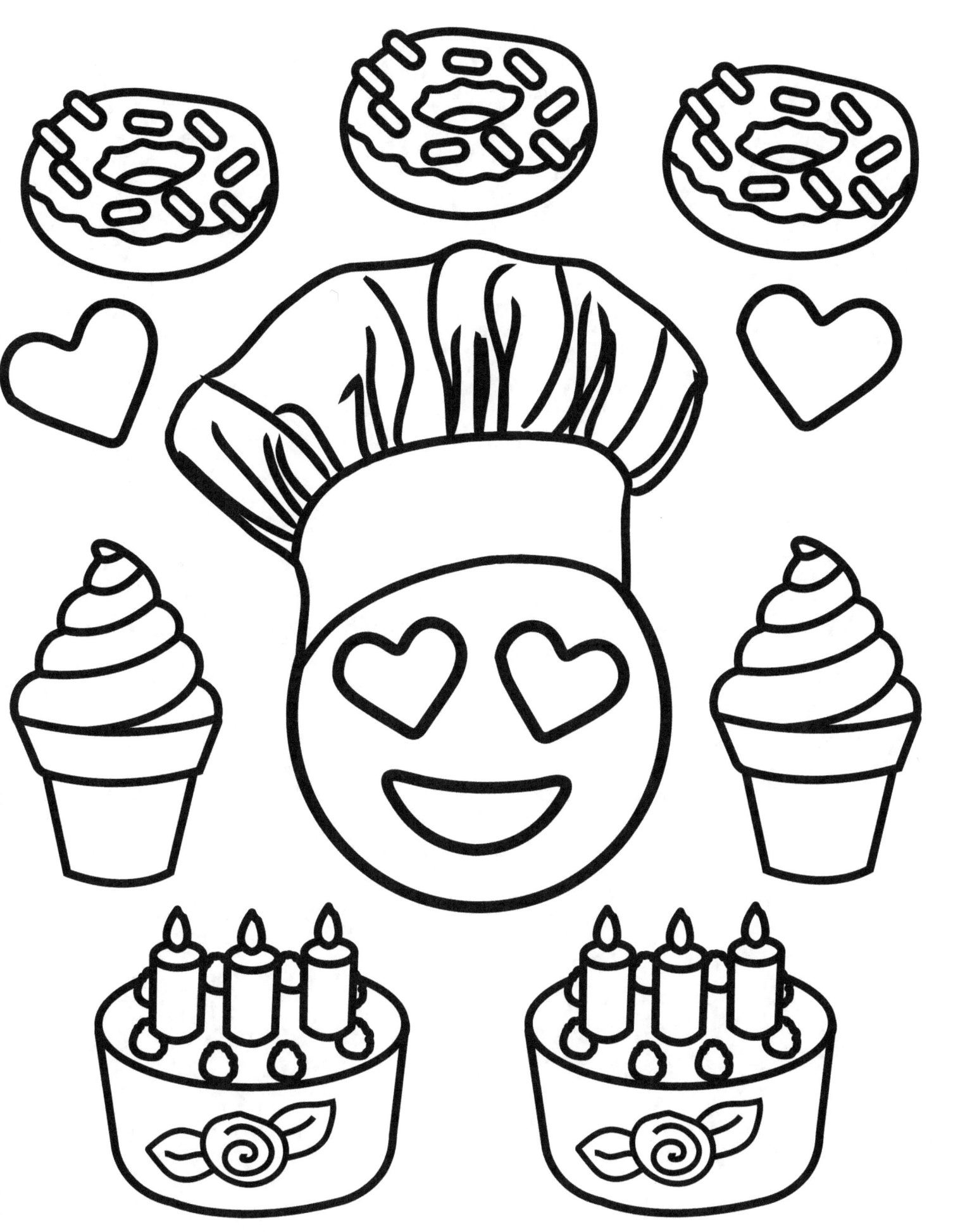

TODAY'S DATE

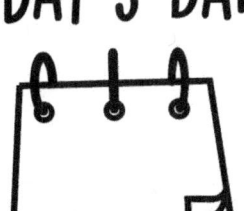

 I WOKE UP FEELING

 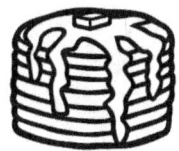  

IN THE AFTERNOON I FELT LIKE:

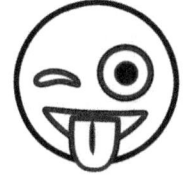  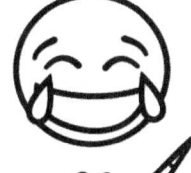

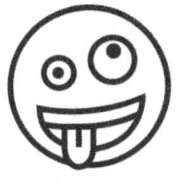  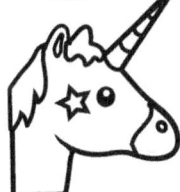

THE WEATHER WAS:

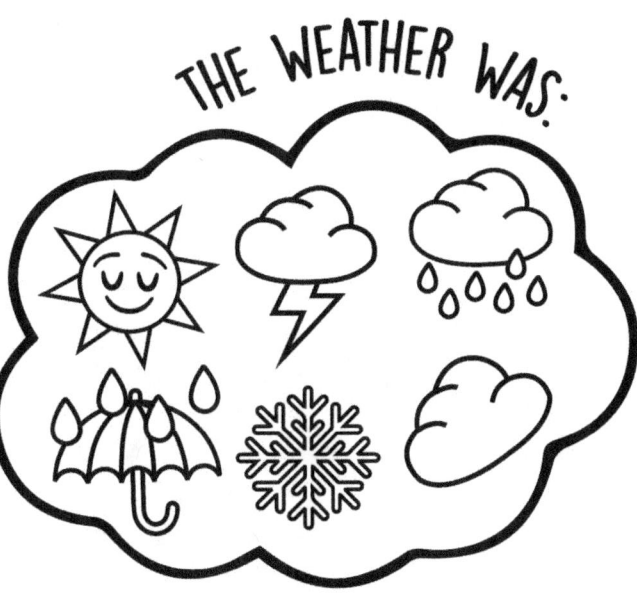

TODAY. . . _____
_____
_____
_____
_____
_____
_____
_____

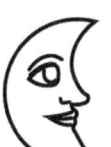 NIGHT TIME MOOD: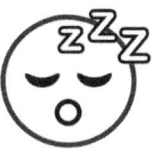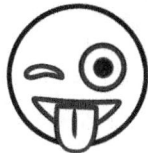

MOVIE NIGHT

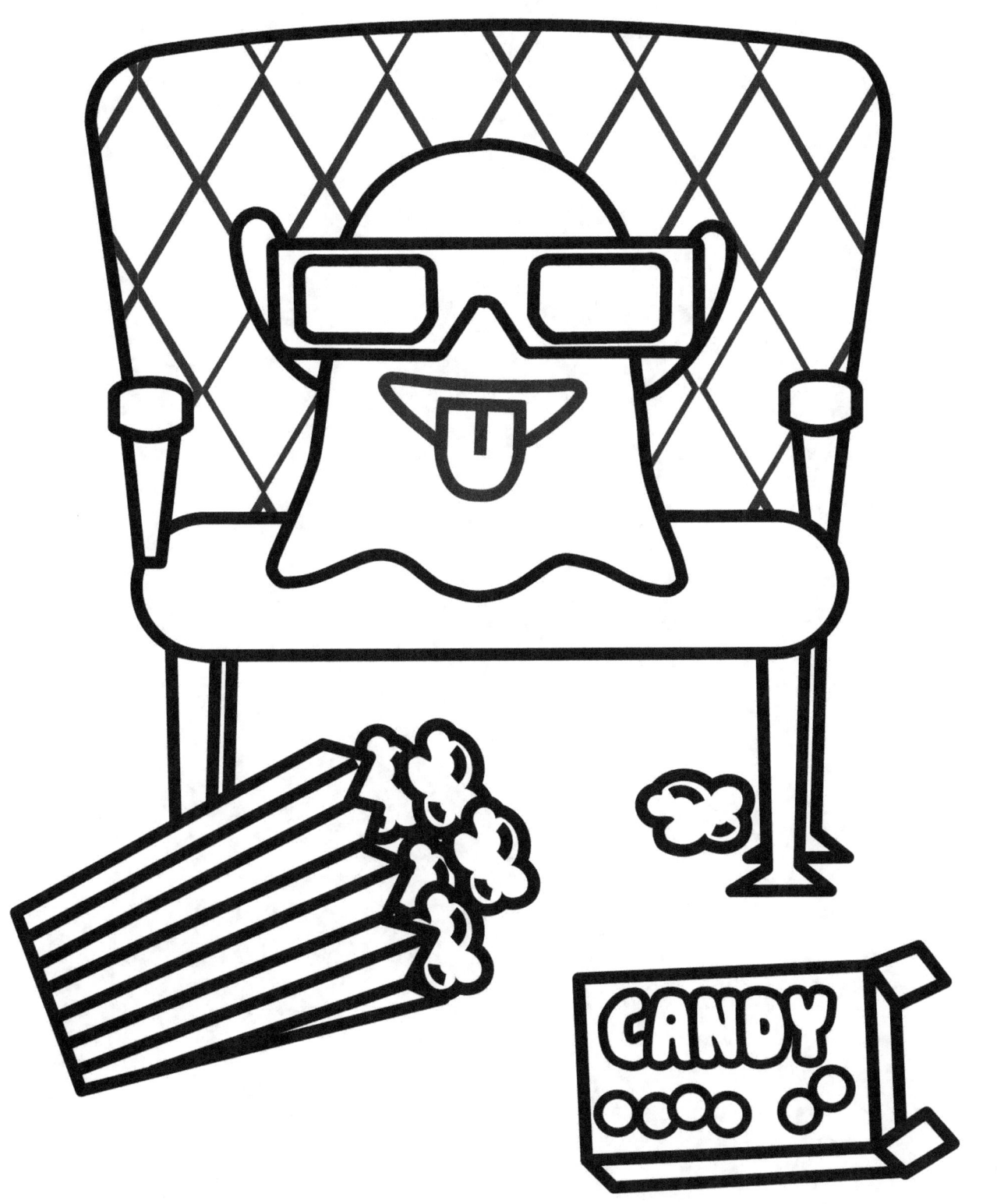

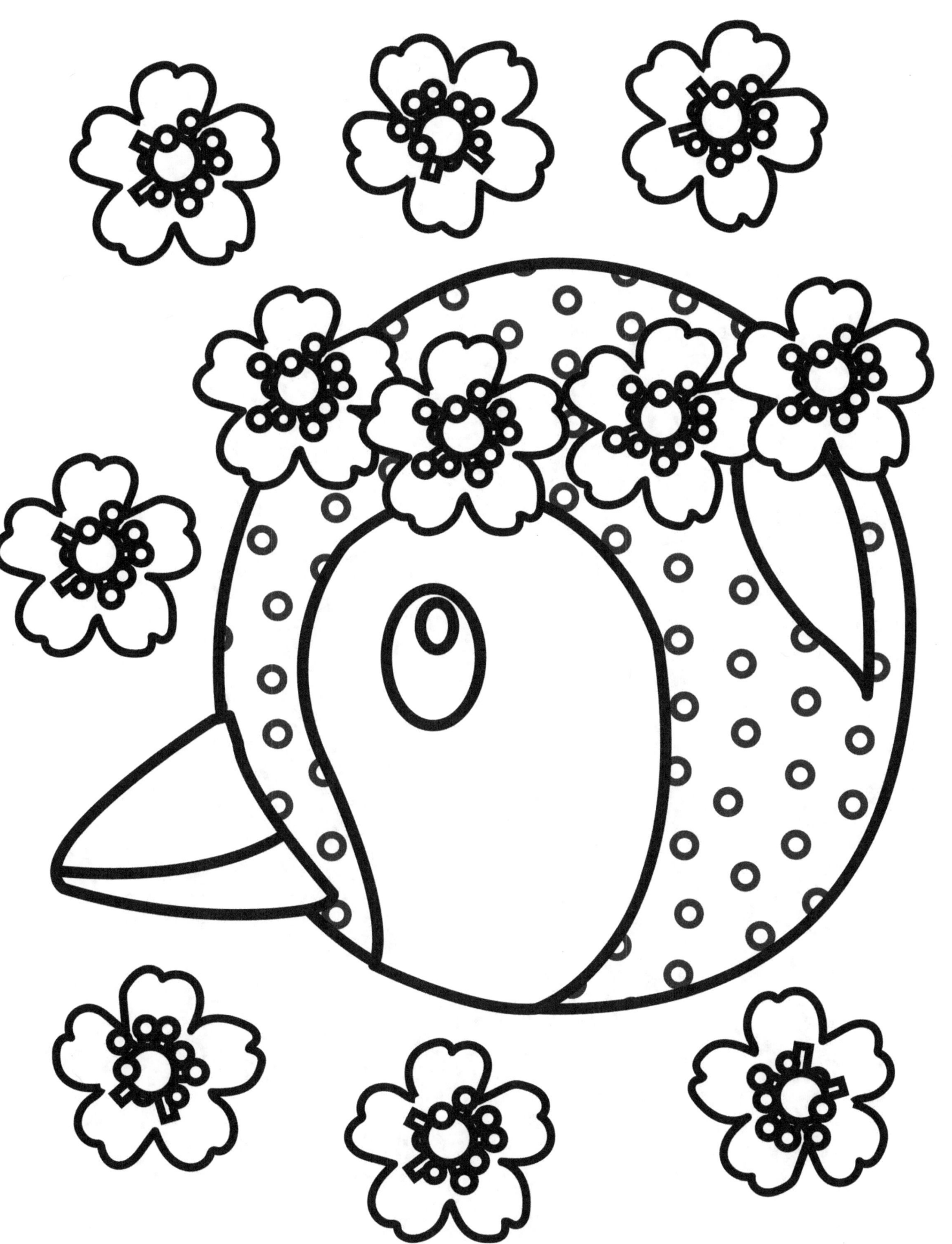

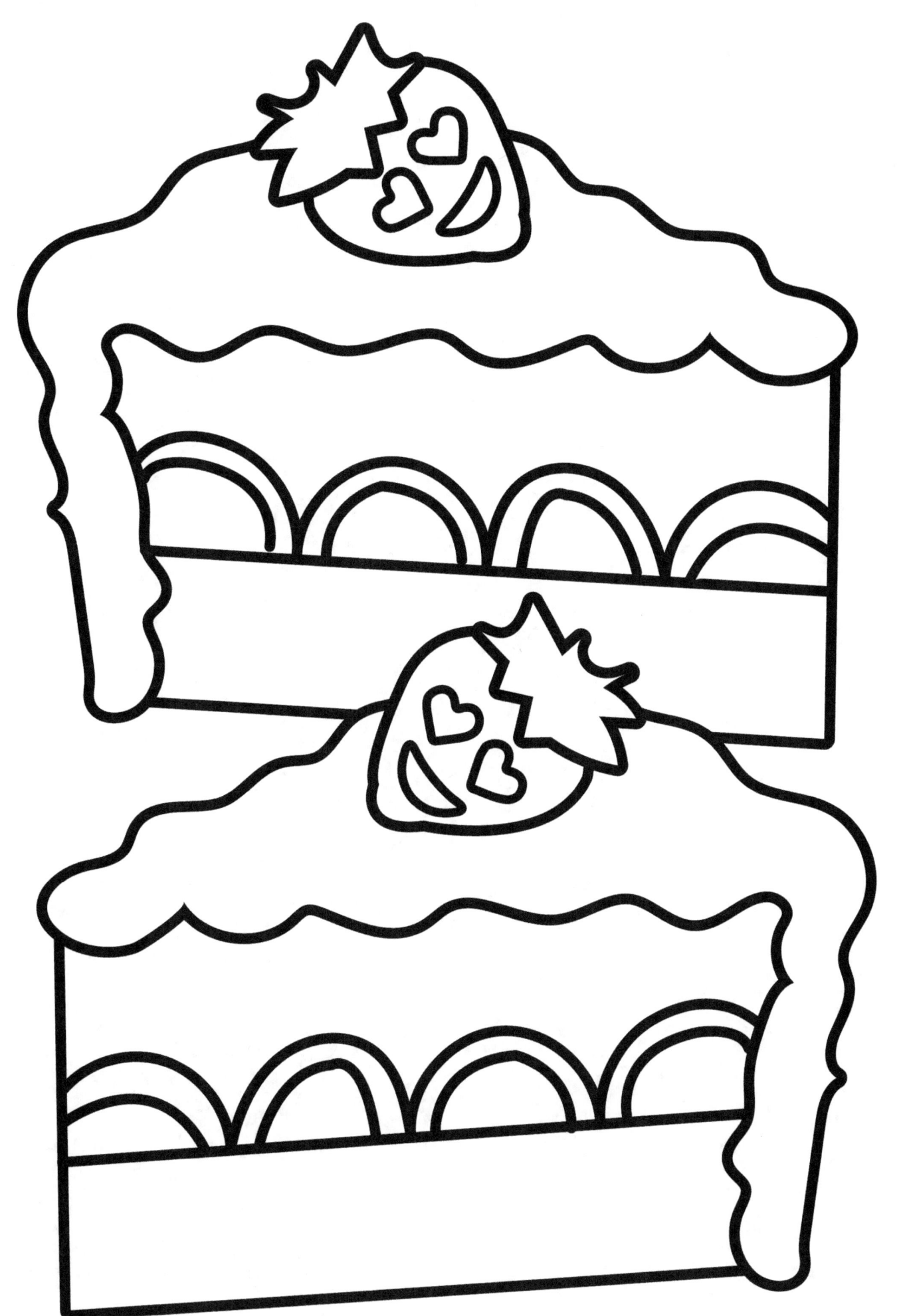

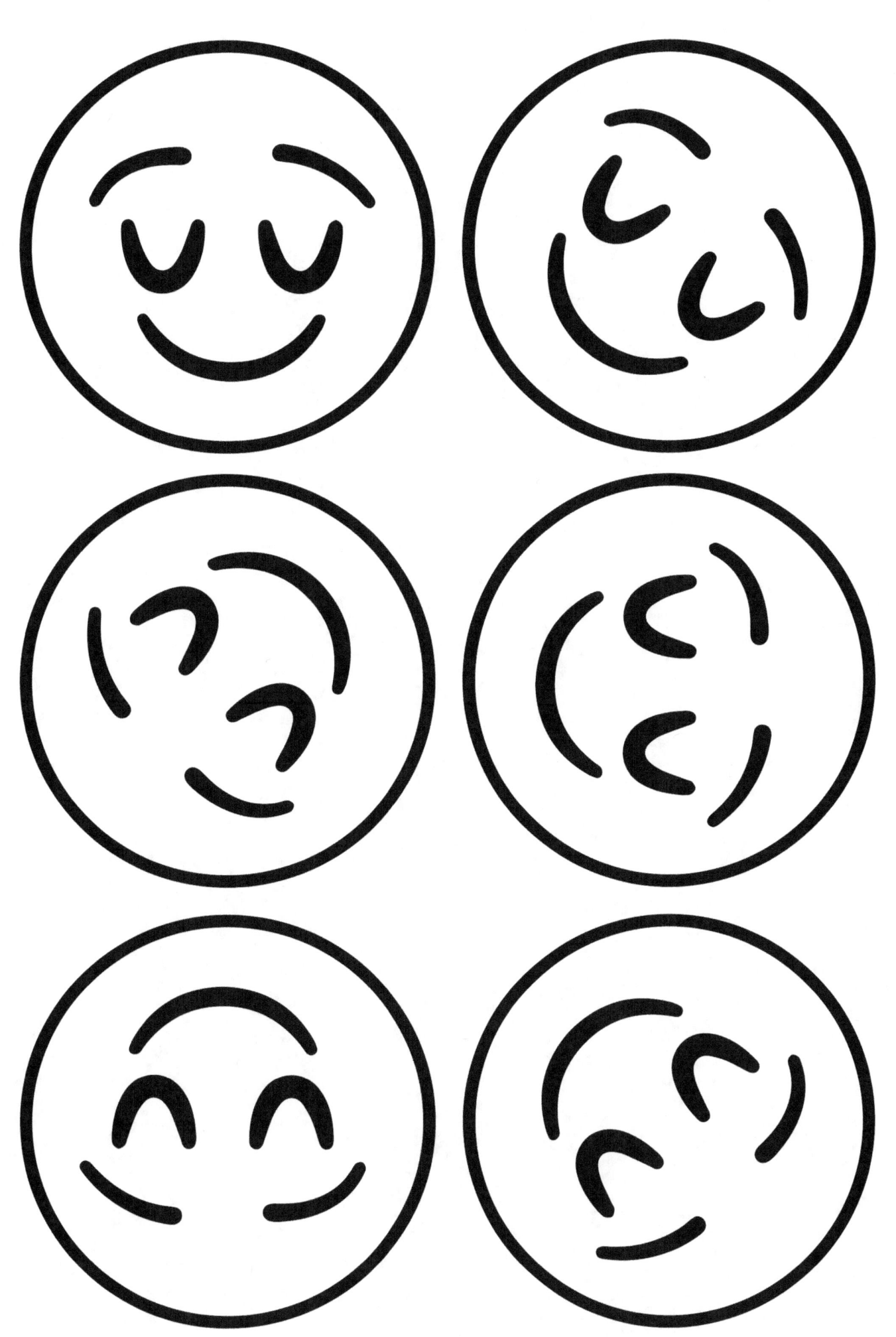

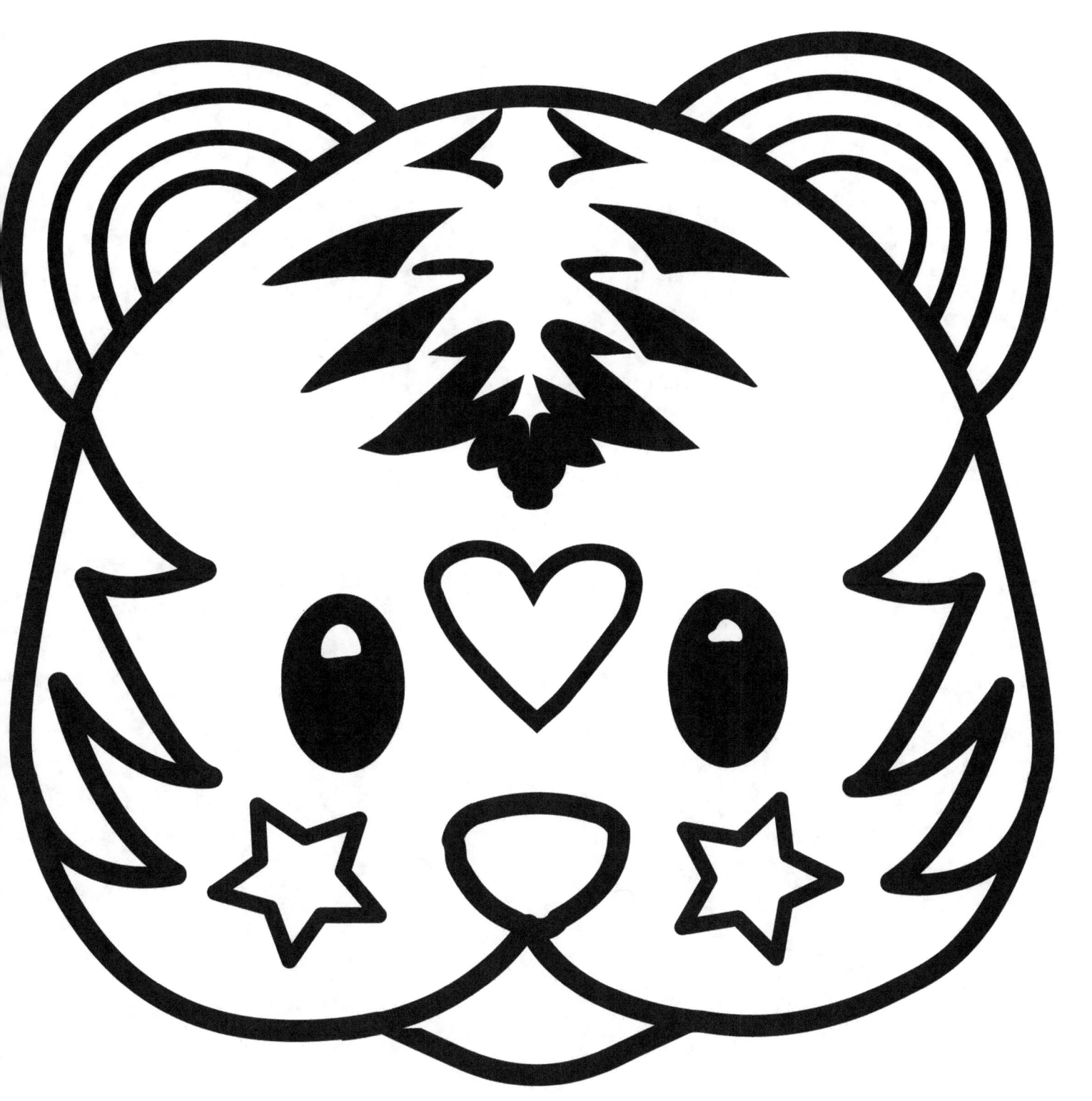

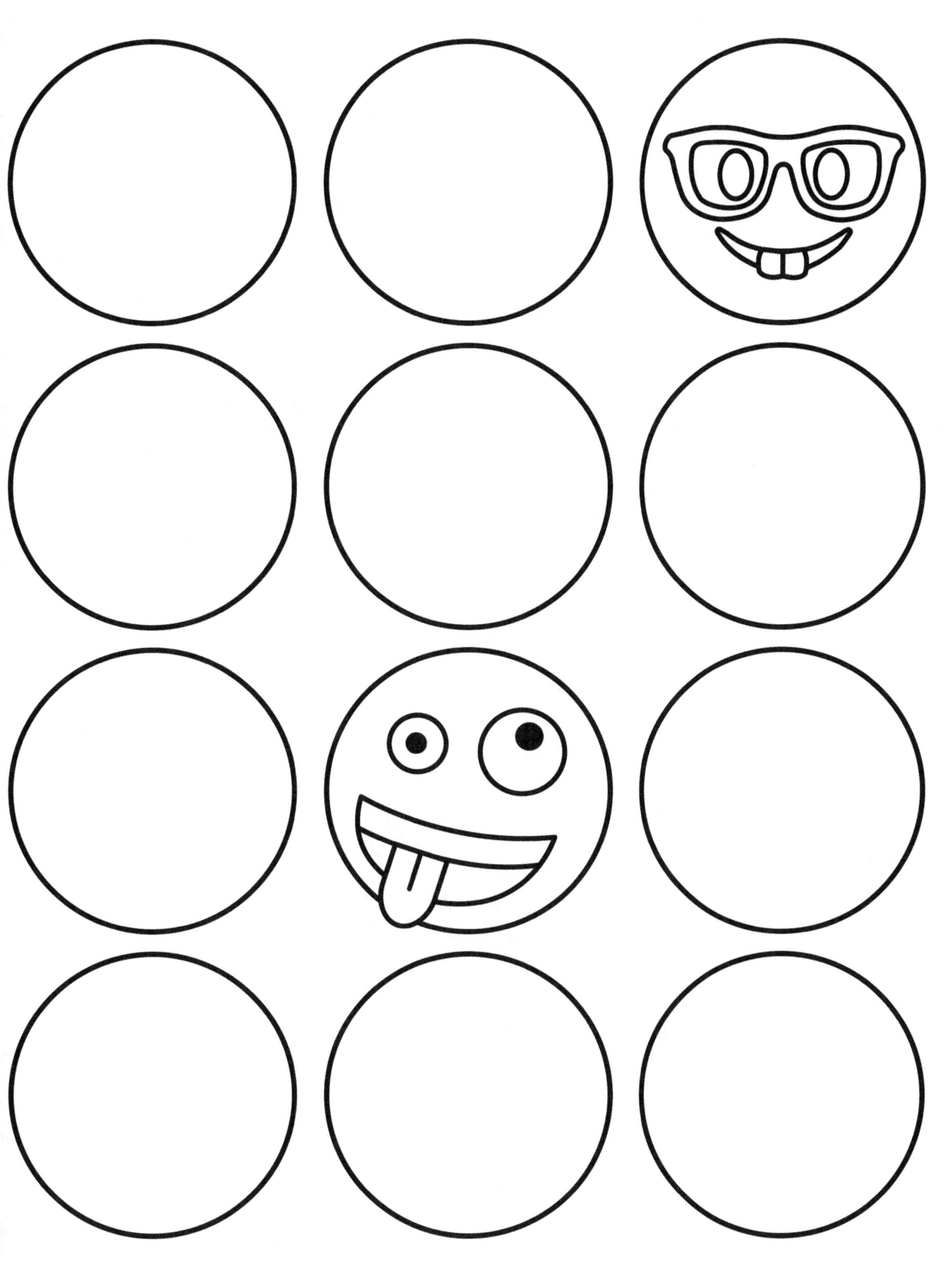